THE OTHER SIDE OF GROWING OLDER

Pat Brown, SRN, SCM, HVC, FWTC

Illustrated by
Gillian Simmonds, ARCA

M

First published 1982 by
THE MACMILLAN PRESS LTD
London and Basingstoke
Companies and representatives throughout the world

Printed in Hong Kong

ISBN   0   333   32313   0 (hard cover)
       0   333   32314   9 (paper cover)

The Other Side of Growing Olde

The 'New Approaches to Care' Series

Patients are people. They have feelings, families and fears. Whatever the cause for their seeking help, the caring professional will find that he or she will be concerned with these other issues. All illness carries with it anxiety and each person has very individual and important feelings about it; feelings which can easily be forgotten or neglected when nurses become preoccupied with the details of treatments, procedures and ward routines.

The 'New Approaches to Care' Series aims to explore this 'other side' of care in a practical and realistic way, emphasising the importance of meeting all the patients' needs, whilst recognising the constraints and problems which so often make the 'other side' the forgotten side of patient care.

The books in this series examine the implications that treatments, procedures, investigations and routines can have for patients and their families. They also aim to help nurses gain some insight into the problems, feelings and anxieties which people can experience when they are being looked after in hospital or the community. The series will thus offer a tangible starting point for all nurses and other professionals, both in training and in practice, to give their patients the most complete and understanding care possible.

Series Editors

June Jolly, SRN, RSCN has devoted most of her nursing career to the care of sick children, and was involved with establishing a new paediatric unit at Brook General Hospital, Woolwich.

Jill Macleod Clark, BSc, PhD, SRN is a Lecturer in the Department of Nursing Studies, Chelsea College, University of London.

Will Bridge, BSc, PhD is the Co-ordinator of the Learning Resources Unit at Brighton Polytechnic.

Contents

Foreword

In dealing with people of any age — young, middle-aged or elderly — it is essential to remember that they are indivduals and to resist any temptation to typecast them. Probably it is even more important to recognise and respect the individuality of the elderly person than of the teenager, because we who have reached or passed our 'allotted span' are less malleable.

Age is relative. We all know this. We all know, too, that 'you're only as old as you feel'. But sometimes it needs a jolt to make us realise that all such truisms are *true*. It was a shock when I first heard myself described by a younger colleague as 'the doyenne of women's page journalists'. It was a shock of a pleasanter kind when the 80-year-old mother of a friend hearing about my numerous activities said fondly 'What it is to be young', for I was then almost 60. And, when at the age of nearly 75 I was invited to give a talk on 'The View of an Elderly Person', I burst out laughing. What me? An elderly person? No, it's the others who are old, and even elderly. I am *me*.

The elderly are not necessarily rigid in their thinking or impervious to new impressions and ideas, but their personalities have been formed by years of living and it is too much to expect them to fit easily or willingly into formal patterns of life devised by other, younger people for administrative convenience. We really should not expect the old lady who has run her own home for 50 to 60 years to accept without distress the idea of sharing a bedroom in an 'old folks' home' with two or three total strangers. We cannot expect her to enjoy being called 'Gran' by all and sundry, even though she may smile at the good-natured ambulance man or hospital orderly who uses it almost as a term of endearment. We certainly cannot expect her to feel anything but outrage at being classified as a 'geriatric'.

The rapid increase in the proportion of elderly and really old people in our population makes consideration of their needs and how to meet them imperative and urgent. But there is a danger in this concentration of attention on the older age groups — that they be lumped together in a 'problem category'. Certainly people of retirement age have problems — so do people of any age — but Mr *A*'s problem may be arthritic joints, Mrs *B*'s of loneliness following widowhood, and Miss *C*'s and the Rev *D*'s where to live after retiring from 'residential' jobs. It is the problems that the carers need to think out and to deal with, rather than the age.

Pat Brown's book is especially welcome because she deals with such a wide range of the problems of older people. It is still more valuable because of its straightforward jargon-free writing. Here is none of that sociological gobbledegook in which some writers on social problems wrap up their thoughts. She never uses phrases like 'service input' or 'radical welfare pluralism', but sticks to the simple straightforward language which is as meaningful to the 'cared for' as to the 'carer'. Her language is an expression of her sympathetic approach. Sociological jargon tends to condition the thinking of the person who uses it, and to distance the trained person from the 'customer'.

To me one of Pat Brown's most important insights is into the difference between the 'young old' and the 'old old' — the two groups cannot, of course, be defined solely by age, but a rough and ready demarcation is between the 60 to 75-year-olds and the over 75s. Politicians, civil servants, trade unionists and, most of all, the elderly themselves, should devote more thought to what can be expected of, and what can be provided for, the 'young old' in comparison with the 'old old'. Even as things are, the 'young old' should not be regarded as a burden on society, but rather as a resource, but if, as we must expect, the age of retirement is lowered, partly because of the economic recession and also because of changes in technology which means fewer people are needed to provide sufficient goods and services, a sizable proportion of our population may be pensioners for as much as 30 years, or one third of their life span. Only a teenager or a newly wed would think of a person of 55 as 'old'. Yet if people are retired on pension at that age they will inevitably be lumped in with the 'OAP's' and 'senior citizens' — unless society develops a new set of attitudes towards what we ought now to start calling the 'third age' — and indeed towards what retirement is and what it entails. The attitude of the trade unions still tends to be that forty or more years of hard work and of statutory contributions to the health service and pension funds have earned the worker honorable and well-supported retirement from daily, paid employment. Pat Brown is well aware of the many ways in which the brains, experience and energy of the newly retired can be harnessed and used for the common good, and the good of the pensioners themselves.

As Pat Brown and similarly concerned and caring nurses and social workers fully realise, activity is essential to health and well-being. There has been a lot of discussion in the last year or two of the need to take a new look at 'the work ethic'. Can men and women live happily without commitment to work — a job which, paid or unpaid, has to be done? I doubt it. One has known too many men who have lost heart and interest in life and died young when their paid employment ceased. (One of the reasons why women live longer than men is almost certainly that they continue to work by keeping the home going, etc. even if they are retired from business or the professions.)

So the job of all 'carers', it seems to me, whether they are social workers, nurses or trade union officials, is to encourage the ageing to think of themselves as useful citizens who can earn the respect and gratitude of their fellow men and women by engaging in some voluntary activity. The great enemy of the ageing, as of the bereaved, is self-pity. I know this from the traumatic experience of being suddenly widowed, when I had to keep reminding myself, day after day, that there was always someone worse off, someone more to be pitied. This is true of being old, ill and poor as well as of being bereaved, and it is not for the friendly, healthy, well-provided-for young social worker or nurse to say 'Snap out of it Mrs *A*' or Mr *B*'. But I think it would be possible sometimes to drop a hint that Mrs *A* and Mr *B* might lend a hand to a crippled or confused neighbour — because it makes *them* feel good to be in a better command of their faculties than Mrs *X* and Mr *Y*.

I personally am grateful to Pat Brown for bravely tackling the question of dying and death itself. Naturally and properly most younger people revolt against any discussion of death. But we who are 70 and over, know that our time is running out. It is right that we should be helped to think about how the end may come and how our beloved sons and daughters will cope? One of the most memorable things in Pat Brown's book is her story of Mr Richards, terminally ill with cancer, who finally lashed out with 'Why didn't you tell me the truth? God knows I asked often enough'. 'Why is it', asks Pat Brown, 'that so few of us can talk of death to the dying?' Her answer is that it is due to 'embarrassment due to the failure to cure the patient'. I think it is also due to the fact that, unlike our Victorian ancestors, we have grown up regarding death as a taboo subject.

I can discuss death easily and even cheerfully with my 97-year-old friend Gertrude. If a younger person heard us, even the most caring and concerned nurse, she would say, 'Now really, you don't want to talk about morbid things like that'. But it is not morbid for old people to learn to face the inevitability of the future. If only we could be helped to think of death as a doorway, how much less fearful we all might be.

Mary Stott, OBE

Acknowledgements

This book would never have come about if it had not been for the energy, enthusiasm and stamina of June Jolly and Jill Macleod Clark. It was they who first suggested the book, it was they who convinced me that I was capable of writing it, and they, with Will Bridge, have had the horrendous job of sub-editing it. In everything, except the royalties, the book is as much theirs as mine.

My thanks to Gillian Simmons for her intuitive illustrations and to Norman, my husband, for remembering who I was on the odd occasions he saw me during the writing process. My gratitude to les Girls who managed to convert my atrocious handwriting and typewriting into legible scripts — to Sue Sycamore, Peggy Painter, Jackie Fane and Theresa Down — thank you for all your help and patience.

Without library facilities it would be impossible to write any book and I am indebted to Susan Merriott, District Medical Librarian, Worthing, and to David Rae, Librarian, Brighton Polytechnic, Falmer, and also to Maureen Fraser for the use of her extensive private library.

Most of all my grateful thanks to all the people who over the years have allowed me into their homes and into their confidence. To all the 'characters' and eccentrics who have delighted me and others — long may they all continue.

Introduction

This is not just another book about nursing geriatric patients. It is about what happens when people grow old — it is about old age and the process of ageing; about society's attitudes to ageing; and about the myths and realities of old age. Old age is simply an extension of middle age — it is to be hoped that growing old is one thing that will happen to us all, because if you don't get old you're going to die young, and most of us look forward to a bit of enjoyable retirement after our working life.

The aim of this book is to explore all aspects of old age in the hope that a better understanding of the complexities and problems will result in the provision of better care. This book is intended primarily for the caring professions, especially those people working in the community, because that is where the action is. It is also written for everyone who is caring for an elderly person, whether they are relatives, friends or patients in hospital. And finally, this book is for the elderly themselves, in the hope that it will provide them with information, advice and enthusiasm for this time of life.

In the first part of the book an attempt is made to put growing old into perspective. In chapters 1 - 3 some of the facts and figures related to the elderly are examined; how many there are in the population, where they live, and the physical and psychological effects of ageing. The topic of retirement is analysed in detail and some of the commonly held misconceptions about ageing are explored. The next four chapters of the book examine some of the problems encountered in old age — problems of dependency, incontinence, alcoholism, vulnerability and loneliness. The very common problems of confusion and eccentricity are also explored in detail, using many anecdotes from the author's own experience as a community nurse.

Chapter 8 tackles the subject of death and bereavement in the elderly, and in the final chapter many suggestions are made for important changes in our current health care provision — changes which would benefit both the elderly population and those who care for them.

The funny thing about age is that it is a thing that usually happens to 'other people'. We notice how our friends, our relatives and our work colleagues are ageing and tend to make the following type of remark: 'Poor old Tom looks a bit haggard. I wonder when he retires. Can't be long now, he looks as if he ought to have gone years ago' or 'Have you noticed how grey Mary is getting? She's looking her age.

Of course, she's getting on'.

Our mirrors are much kinder to ourselves; we see little change as the years go by. We feel very little different from how we felt last year, perhaps a bit stiffer than we were 20 years ago, but not really very much. So when do we grow old? To an 18 year old anyone over 40 has more or less had it. The 40 year old probably thinks that people over 70 are getting on a bit, but the 70 year old enjoying his pint, his bowls, his darts or his garden would laugh at the idea that he is elderly or old.

Then when do we cross the magic dateline? When are we old? Is it on the day we first draw our old age pension, now thankfully referred to as the retirement pension, or is it on the day we get to 70, or 80, or 90?

To the majority of retired people age is a matter of dependence. You are not old while you are independent. They talk of 'poor old people' meaning people who need outside help to maintain their way of life. How many times have we heard someone say of a club or a residential home, 'I won't go there any more, it's full of old people'?

If we age in proportion to the amount of support needed, then the vast majority of our retired population are not old. They might be getting on a bit, they might even be creaking in the odd joint, but they are enjoying their lives without needing or requesting help from the statutory or voluntary organisations.

Ageing then is a gradual process. We all get older every day — in fact you have aged a minute or so while you have been reading this far. If the prospect of getting old frightens us, and there is no reason in the world why it should, then we might look at the sort of provision that we have made for our aged population. Is what we do for them today good enough for us tomorrow? If the system worries us, then we had better get the system right before we become part of it.

Everyone involved in caring for the elderly *must* accept that age is not an affliction, that just because someone is over 80 years of age does not mean that they are mindless idiots. It is also important to remember that the dependent elderly comprise a very small proportion of the population.

We might then be able to get the needs of the dependent elderly more in perspective and be able to utilise the tremendous amount of willing voluntary help which is available from the retired independent population. And if all that happens we might be able to give better care.

1 The Elderly —
Some Facts and Figures

Old age is when you first realise other people's faults are no worse
than your own

Edgar A. Shoaff (see Peter, 1977)

Introduction

There is a pattern to life. We are born, we grow up, we
grow old and we die. That seems very simple and very basic,
but what complicates it are factors which affect this life
cycle, such as where we are born, who our parents are,
their social class, the colour of their skins, religion, and how
civilised or uncivilised the society we are born into happens
to be. We hope that, for the majority of us, our pattern of
life will evolve within and around our family or group.
That is certainly where we would wish our child bearing,
child rearing, growing up, growing old and dying to take
place. This chapter looks at some rather bold facts about
growing old in our society.

Who are the Elderly?

According to British government statistics 'the elderly'
are all those over 65 years (60 for women), and wherever
statistics are quoted in this book that is the age range being
considered. However, most of us would probably tend
to equate 'elderly' with those over 75-80 years and think
of 'the retired' as the active, fit, independent people up
to 75-80. Dependency, and certainly extreme dependency,
brings with it an almost automatic connotation of being old
or elderly.

Whatever name is applied to those who are past middle
life, be it 'the old', 'the aged', 'the older generation', 'the

elderly', 'senior   citizens', 'pensioners', 'the retired' or the particularly distasteful 'golden oldies', the label is bound to offend someone.

The other thing to be aware of is the misuse of the term 'geriatrics'. To qualify as a 'geriatric' one must be over 65 years, ill, and being treated by a hospital geriatric department. You can be 80 years old and on an orthopaedic ward and you will be an orthopaedic patient; if you are on a surgical ward you will be a surgical patient; admission at any age to a medical ward will make you a medical patient; but if you are admitted to a geriatric ward, you become a 'geriatric'. However, it is a pity that the word 'geriatrics' is seen by many people in a derogatory light. It is as much a speciality as paediatrics or any other branch of medicine. Modern geriatric departments can pride themselves on the skill, compassion and understanding that they bring to the treatment of patients over 65.

Another word which is entering our vocabulary from the United States is 'gerontology'. Gerontology is the scientific study of ageing and the problems associated with it. It takes in a very wide field. It looks at the social, environmental, economic, physiological and psychological aspects of ageing and their effects on the aged. Geriatrics is that part of gerontology that deals with the prevention and treatment of disease in old people. As a geriatrician recently told me, 'Twenty years ago, if we got you, we kept you in cold storage for the undertaker. Now we cure you and send you home. That's modern geriatrics.'

Historical Perspectives

Home is the best place to grow old. It is certainly the best place to die and it is always the best place to live. From the beginning of time, caring for those unable to care for themselves has been a family or group commitment and society has always looked to the family as the caring unit. The Poor Law Act of 1601 stated:

And be it further enacted, that the father and grandfather and the mother and grandmother, and the children of

every poor, old, blind, lame and impotent person, or other
person not able to work, being of a sufficient ability,
shall at their own charge relieve and maintain every such
poor person.

Those who had no family had to fall back on the 'parish'
and later the 'workhouse'. Poverty was seen as indolence,
improvidence and even vice. Today we still talk about the
unemployed as being shiftless, lazy and idle.

Three hundred years later the Poor Law Act of 1930
again emphasized the family commitment:

It shall be the duty of the father, grandfather, mother,
grandmother, husband or child, of a poor, old, blind, lame
or impotent person, or other poor person able to work,
if possessed of sufficient means, to relieve and maintain
that person.

Most people, in times of stress, need the familiar things of
home about them. This is particularly important to the very
young and the very old. Although there is no longer a legal
duty on families to care, the moral obligation is still accepted
by most of them.

Many factors have changed the pattern of family life —
factors such as the increase in life expectancy, the increased
mobility of the population, the easy availability of
contraception, the higher levels of employment amongst
women, and inflation, particularly the cost of housing.
Improvements in environmental health, immunisation against
infectious diseases, better school health services, less poverty,
improvements in medicine, advances in surgery and the vast
improvements in drug therapy have all led to an increase in
life expectancy. People move about a lot more now and
families become scattered through migration and emigration.
Our great grandparents went to market once a month, but
our children think nothing of global travel. Young people
move because of work opportunities, and may marry and
settle far away from their parents.

The development of Family Planning Clinics throughout

the country has seen a decrease in the number of children born, so there are less children around to care for the older generations. With fewer children, and their child-bearing and child-rearing condensed into a shorter period of their lives, women are now more likely to be a part of the workforce and, therefore, are not available to look after their parents. Soaring property costs and the shrinking size of the homes now being built have also played their part. The new estates of little coloured boxes have little room for the older generation. The familiar patterns are changing. We have moved away from the old extended family with its kinship ties spreading through generations like the branches of the well-known chestnut tree, towards a smaller nuclear type family with its regulation 2.2 children. But, although the patterns are changing, there is nothing to indicate that the family ties of love, respect and duty are any less significant today than they were in the past.

The Proportion of Elderly in the Population

As discussed previously, the average person now lives longer: as a result there are more elderly people and the number of retired people in the country has risen in proportion to the rest of the population. Every book and every article written about the elderly refers to the rise in numbers as if the whole balance of nature was about to be disturbed.

The following table shows the number of retired persons in the United Kingdom as a percentage of the population for selected years (data after Owen, 1976):

Year	Percentage
1965	12.2
1975	14.1
1985	14.7
1995	14.4

When you look at the above statistics, all they really say is that by 1995 there will be 2 per cent more retired people in the population than there were in 1965. In 1965, on average, 12 out of every 100 people had retired and in 1995 an average of 14 out of every 100 people will have retired. So there will be a few more of us about, but it does not mean that as a country we are suddenly going to be over-run by elderly Zimmer-waving octogenarians.

For the first time in history we can say that the biblical expectation of three-score years and ten has been reached; the average life expectancy is now 70-77 years and by the year 2050 it is expected to have reached 85 years. So not only are more of us living to retirement age, but we are now hanging about a lot longer when we get there. This is very pleasant for those of us who manage to make it, but it seems to be giving the planners of the future an awful headache as regards what to do with us.

Where the Elderly Live

Another hoary old chestnut is that 'families no longer care for their elderly', but Arie (1975) says,

> At any one time, in round figures, 94% of people over 65 years are at home, 1% are in general hospitals, 1% are in geriatric hospitals, 1% are in mental hospitals, 2% are in old people's homes and 1% are in various other places. The 3% in hospitals account for nearly half the beds in the NHS.

Our colleagues caring for patients in hospitals may feel that all old people are ill and dependent because all the old people they see or treat are of necessity ill and dependent. However, as we can see from the statistics, the number of elderly patients in hospital form a minute proportion of the retired population. Approximately 94 per cent of the elderly are living at home, and according to the HMSO Health and Personal Social Services Statistics for England (1975) 70 per cent of these are living with their families.

The residential environment of persons over 65 years of age in the UK can be summarised by the pie diagram shown overleaf.

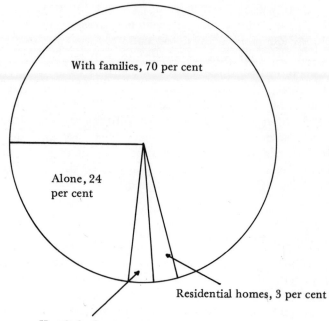

With families, 70 per cent

Alone, 24
per cent

Residential homes, 3 per cent

Hospitals, 3 per cent

So it seems that families *do* still care. Some families shoulder intolerable burdens and strain for years. Elderly husbands and wives care for each other with a devotion that is sometimes heroic. Sons and daughters take their parents into their homes to look after them. It is not to be wondered if at times the situation breaks down. The carer can become ill with the strain of 24 hour nursing over many years, and we must never forget that age does not always bring serenity and that some old people may be just a little difficult to get on with. One 60 year old daughter, who had looked after her 90 year old mother for years, told me that her mother was a 'b-minded old fuss-pot' and that the only way the daughter could cope was to get out and dig the garden. She had the best dug garden for miles around – but she continued to care for the old lady until she died.

THOSE WHO ARE OLD AND ALONE

We know that something like a quarter of all old people actually do live on their own. However, the term 'living alone' brings to mind elderly semi-invalids, struggling on their own to get the basic ingredients of life, such as food, water, heat and light. Make no mistake, there are still plenty of people living in our society doing just that, but a large percentage of the retired people who live alone do so out of choice and not necessity. We must always remember that the vast majority of the retired population, many of them only in their 60s and 70s, are fit, active, healthy people. It must be recognised that being alone and being lonely are two quite different things.

THOSE IN HOMES

Only a small percentage of the elderly population (about 3 per cent) actually require or choose residential care. For them the choice of accommodation is as wide as it is unpredictable. People who need residential care will probably be the very elderly members of our society. They will be the frail elderly and handicapped elderly who can no longer cope on their own. The choice of homes lies between the state-run homes, the voluntary or charitable homes and the private sector. My suggestion to all those elderly people contemplating such a move — and to their families — is *take advice*. Ask the local health and social services departments for information and help. Go and have a look at the homes, and ensure that if possible the person concerned is given a chance to go and live in one for a few weeks. Find out what you are committing yourself to. Time spent in reconnaissance is seldom wasted. (See the section in chapter 4 entitled 'They'd be far better off in a home'.)

The Migratory Patterns of the Elderly

It has been recognised for some time that mobility of labour brings with it isolation of the family. As one woman put it,

We only have two children. Helen, our girl, is in Canada
with her husband. He has a very good job there. Tom,
our son, married a lovely Scots girl. They live in
Yorkshire because of his work, so they have no family
near them and we don't see them very often. I feel really
sorry for my daughter-in-law, she has the two children,
a baby and a toddler, and there's none of us near enough
to give her a hand.

Now, it would seem, we have another phenomenon on
our hands, the mobility of the retired population, a
phenomenon which is seen in the USA as well as in the UK.
This mobility takes the form of a migratory exodus towards
a warmer climate: to Florida in the USA and in this country
towards the south coast. There are many reasons for this
lemming-like rush to the sea! There is the obvious advantage
of the warmer climate, the facilities, the sea with its
supposedly health-giving properties, and the many clubs
geared to the older person and the slower pace of life. However, life may not quite live up to expectations when the
elderly arrive at a new home. Increased longevity, earlier
retirement, better pensions and the desire to enjoy retirement have made many people realise that life can begin
again for them at 60 or 65 years of age. Choice of retirement home can be the result of a life-long desire to move
back to the place of birth, but it is amazing how many
people retire to a place because they have happy memories
of a particularly good holiday there. They were probably
a bit younger, happy in each other's company, the sun
shone, the hotel was welcoming, the food excellent and
everything looked warm and inviting, as it always does
when the sun is shining and we are happy.

What people don't allow for are the disadvantages.
They leave behind the friends of a lifetime, family, clubs,
the local pub, church and their general practitioner. They
move into a new way of life in which they have to make
new friends, get on with new neighbours and find a new
doctor.

Having isolated themselves from their past, couples often
become completely absorbed in each other. When it is

difficult to make new friends they become dependent on each other to an extent that would not have happened in the previous setting. When the inevitable happens and one of them dies, the other one may be left to join the sadly increasing number of isolated, lonely and depressed people, many of whom inhabit the retirement homes on the south coast of England.

The following table indicates the regional and population density distribution of samples of persons aged 65 years and over (from Hunt, 1978):

Standard regions	Percentage of population aged 65 and over
North	6.4
Yorkshire and Humberside	9.8
North-west	14.6
East Midlands and East Anglia	13.5
West Midlands	10.0
Greater London	12.2
South-east and south-west	21.7

Of course not every retired person who moves lives to regret it. Many people enjoy 20 or so good years together in happy and enjoyable harmony. These are the ones who find it easy to join in new activities and may end up doing voluntary service of one kind or another. They are the 'doers' of this world and are capable of looking after themselves in any environment. They are not usually the sort of people who come into contact with the statutory services, and fortunately they are in the majority.

There are a small number of people of all ages who are continually on the move. When they are young or middle-aged it is not so obvious, but once they become really old it becomes noticeable because they tend to need help with the various moves. One very elderly couple I knew took 4 years to move from Scotland to the south coast, stopping along the way for periods of 3-6 months. By the time they got to the coast they were financially impoverished, mentally depressed and as argumentative as any couple I've ever come across. When I asked them why they had left Scotland, they said: 'Because it was so cold and many people had impressed on us that a warmer climate would be better for our arthritis.' So they got down as far as Liverpool.

'And why did you leave Liverpool?' I asked.

'We could not understand the Liverpudlian accent and besides, it was still very cold and the doctor there agreed with us that we would be better off moving south.'

The Midlands had not come up to expectations either, and someone there advised them to continue on down as

well. By the time I saw them they were living in a room that overlooked the sea. While they were telling me the saga of their travels I could not help thinking of the words of the song: 'They've gone about as far as they can go'. What was sad was that having got there, they still weren't any happier.

The Need to Plan and Allocate Resources Appropriately

Now the thing is that people have the right to move anywhere they like, and if they elect to move to a warmer area, or a quieter area, or into or out of the city areas, then surely it is not beyond the imagination of the planners in the various government departments to see that the right resources are available in the right places. It's difficult to know what drives the 'movers' to shift about so frequently, but there's no law that says they can't. It might be administratively more convenient for the statutory services if people allowed themselves to be slotted into spaces and then remained there, but people are not that predictable!

It is obvious that if there is a limited budget and if there are going to be more of us, there will be less to go round in the end. So, what we should be doing, as members of the caring professions, is to shout, loud and clear, to make sure that there is a fairer distribution of the national wealth and that the services to the elderly get properly allocated and funded.

What we need, particularly in the community, is the means to help people to help themselves. More help to families to enable them to carry on caring, and more help for those nearing retiring age to get them ready for retirement. The NHS is one of the biggest employers in the UK, and it is woefully inadequate when it comes to helping its own staff prepare for retirement. Lastly, among the newly retired there is a vast untapped workforce of potential voluntary workers. Not that I would advocate using the retired as unpaid workers, doing jobs for which the state should be paying, but the desire to help one's fellow men and the ability to do something for others has a special reward all of its own.

Physical Effects of Ageing

The normal ageing process produces physical changes, which if unrecognised, untreated and unchecked can lead to a range of physical problems and defects.

VISION

Visual acuity fails gradually for most people after the age of 40, but obviously can be treated by the use of corrective spectacles and contact lenses. As people reach their 80s they will probably find that their retinas are less sensitive to light and they will need to increase the amount of artificial light they use. Old age is not the time for 40 watt bulbs and pulling the curtains to keep the sunlight from fading the furniture! It is the time for allowing as much natural light into the house as possible and for bright artificial light to help lighten the darkness for ageing eyes.

HEARING

Elderly persons' hearing will often become less acute. There may come a time when a hearing aid is needed to lessen the effect of hearing loss. Hearing aids are available free for retired people through the NHS, and consultant appointments are arranged through a patient's GP. The follow-up services such as fitting, having the mould made and getting new aids when they become necessary are usually arranged through the audiology department of the local hospital in association with the GP. Elderly people who feel that their hearing is failing should first visit their GP to make sure that it is not a collection of wax that is causing the hearing loss. One lady of 84, who always carried on her conversations about 40 decibels louder than everyone else, was prevailed upon to go to her GP. He found a 20 year collection of wax that took quite a bit of shifting. Her hearing was so much better afterwards that she had to put cotton wool in her ears for 2 weeks until she could cope with the noise of the traffic!

MOBILITY

Mobility is almost certain to become more restricted in old age, but the process is usually so slow as to be imperceptible. As mobility lessens it is only sensible to remove the things that are likely to cause accidents, including the cosy old rugs, the occasional table full of knick-knacks in the hallway, and the worn stair carpet on poorly lit stairs. Of the thousands of people who die from accidents in their own homes every year, the majority die as a result of falls. Apart from the terrible mortality rate from falls there are many older people who become even more immobile after a fall because their fear of repeating the accident makes them over-cautious.

Effects of Ageing on the Family

Most families are conscientious amd mindful of their elderly relatives. Cresswell and Parker (1972) studied a small group of highly dependent people and found the majority of their carers uncomplaining and heroic. Indeed many times the mistake relatives make is to be over-protective, by performing acts for the elderly which they could and should be doing for themselves. Being over-protective deprives the elderly of much needed exercise, independence and self-esteem. On the other hand, families are often blamed for off-loading elderly relatives because the long previous history of care and self-denial is not known. As nurses and other members of caring teams we should be supporting such families and so avoid these crisis situations.

Effects of Ageing on Society

The elderly have an inevitable impact on society in general. The estimated number of people expected to live into very old age is increasing steadily. For this reason alone the elderly will make greater demands on society in general and on health provision in particular. The estimate is that, by the year 2001, 1 per cent of the population will be over 85 years of age. As this age group are heavy users of all the social services, adequate provision for them is an essential element in any forward planning.

The current shift of emphasis from institutional to community care needs to be monitored by the caring professions. It is not enough to say that people are entitled to live out their lives in their own homes, unless the financial resources are made available to make sure that the care provided is adequate.

Conclusions

The care of people labelled 'elderly', as a proportion of the population, is steadily increasing. This, coupled with social changes, may mean that society in the future will have to look to agencies other than the family for the support of the aged. The fallacy that 'the family no longer cares for its elderly' is still believed by a considerable number of the caring professions, but quite recent studies have shown that this is not so. Families *do* care, and it should be our job to help them to continue to care.

However, before we grow old, there will come for most of us a day that will change our life-style, our routine and the very pattern of our lives — we will retire. We may follow the American pattern and migrate to a warmer area. We may look forward to it, or we may be apprehensive about it. The one thing we should all do as we get nearer to retirement is to think about it.

References

Arie, T. D. H. (1975). UK health needs in a changing setting. In *Health Care in a Changing Setting: the UK Experience*, Ciba Foundation Symposium No. 43 (Eds R. Porter and D. W. Fitzsimons), Elsevier/North Holland Biomedical Press, Amsterdam, p. 92.

Cresswell, J. and Parker, P. (1972). The frail who lead the frail. *New Society*, 20, 407-10.

HMSO (1975); *The Disadvantage of Inequality*, Health and Personal Social Service Statistics, Social Trends No. 5, HMSO, London.

Hunt, A. (1978). *The Elderly at Home*, Office of Population Censuses and Surveys, Social Service Division, London.

Owen, D. (1976). *In Sickness and in Health — The Politics of Medicine*, Quartet Books, London.

Peter, L. (1977). *Quotations for Our Time*, Methuen Paperbacks, London.

Bibliography

Cooper M. H. (1975). *Rationing Health Care,* Croom Helm, London.

Owen, D. (1976). *In Science and Health,* Quartet Books, London.

Townsend, P. (1957). *Family Life of Old People,* Routledge, London.

HMSO (1976). Social Trends No. 7, Central Statistical Office, London.

2 Growing Old is Not So Bad

The end of labour is to gain leisure

Aristotle (384-322 BC)

Introduction

Growing old need not be a time of dismay and withdrawal. Growing old is, for most people, a time to be enjoyed and savoured. Retirement should not be the end, rather the beginning of a different type of life. If you like, a different type of work, but work that is enjoyable — the hobby that we've always longed to devote more time to, the voluntary work that brings its own satisfaction, or just sitting in the garden watching the weeds grow, if that is what gives you pleasure.

There is now a suggestion that because of our increasing elderly population we should have a line drawn between 'the young-old' and 'the old-old'. Already many people in the former group are doing the voluntary work for those in the latter group and they may well be finding in that work a stimulus they never found in their paid careers.

The essentials of retirement are that we have reasonable health, sufficient wealth and a continuing purpose. This chapter explains some of the problems, joys and benefits of retirement and some ways in which the time of retirement can be used to the full are discussed. A selection of the different agencies and resources for the elderly are also explained and described.

You Are as Old as You Feel

Many young people complain that their parents will not accept the fact that they are mature, adult and capable of making their own mistakes. The 17 or 18 year old fumes at the restrictions placed on him by well meaning adults. The 16 year old girl strives optimistically with make-up and clothes to look 19. When we get into the 40s and 50s we are once again in front of the mirror with the make-up and clothes, this time trying to knock a few years off. The balding male tries desperately to cover the bald patch and his wife is probably trying the hormone cream to hide her wrinkles.

We use age to classify people: the 'young man' and the 'old woman'. Getting old is also something that we become afraid of because the back half of life, with all its imagined horrors, is looming. Whereas in youth the years drag, in old age they seem to race away. But the compensating factor is that we never feel that we age as much, or as quickly, as do those around us. They may look their age but deep down inside we don't feel any different. We don't suddenly wake up one morning and say. 'This is my 65th birthday, I am now retired, so I am old'. They say that inside every old person is a young person trying to get out. Or as the following anonymous author puts it,

You tell me I am getting old. I tell you that's not so.
The 'house' I live in is worn out and that, of course, I
    know.
It's been in use a long, long while; it's weathered many a
    gale;
I'm really not surprised you think it's getting somewhat
    frail.
The colour's changing on the roof, the window's getting
    dim.
The wall's a bit transparent and looking rather thin.
The foundation's not so steady as once it used to be.
My 'house' is getting shaky but my 'house' isn't me.

My few short years can't make me old. I feel I'm in my
    youth.
Eternity lies just ahead, a life of joy and truth.
I'm going to live forever there, life will go on — it's grand.
You tell me I am getting old. You just don't understand.
The dweller in my little 'house' is young and bright and
    gay;
Just starting on a life to last throughout eternal day.
You only see the outside, which is all that most folks see.

You tell me I'm getting old, you've mixed my 'house' with
me!

So the problem is that many people never see or think of
themselves as old. What is so easy to see in other people is
difficult to relate to ourselves. People whom we consider old
or elderly are continually surprised and annoyed at our interpretation of their ageing. Particularly if we equate age with
inability: 'I don't think it is advisable to use that step-ladder
at your age.'
  In a recent study, Luker (1981) investigated the opinions
of elderly women regarding the benefits of visits by health
visitors. Of the women interviewed, 95 per cent had enjoyed
the visits. However, 53 per cent considered that there were
persons worse off than themselves who were in more need of
health visitor services; this is termed the 'somebody worse
than me' syndrome. Luker suggests that this syndrome

> might be the way that elderly people cope with growing
> older in that as long as they believe that there are people in
> the world worse off than themselves they are able to cope
> effectively with the restrictions that old age eventually
> imposes on daily life.

It is not that they set out intentionally to fool people about
their increasing age, it is just that they never feel as old as
they look to us. Just as we never feel as old as we look to
people 20 years younger. Their 'house' may be getting older
but inside they continue to be young and bright and gay.
  Conversely, after about the age of 90, elderly people
sometimes develop the 'aren't I clever to have got this far'
syndrome. They can afford to boast about their healthy antecedents and about their own stamina. They take pride in
the 'survival of the fittest' theory and point out to anyone
who is interested that they have outlived the rest of their
generation. It is at this point that they occasionally start
adding the years on again. They hardly ever say, 'I'm 94 years
old', instead they will say, 'I'm in my 95th year'. Sometimes
they add a few years on for effect: 'Oh, yes, another year or
so and I'll be getting my telegram from the Queen'.
  In life, as in most things it is the quality, not the quantity,

that is all important. Classification of age is meaningless; we should be looking at capabilities, not counting the wrinkles. Modern gerontology should be gearing itself to improving the quality of the years we have, not looking to extend our time beyond a useful and independent retirement.

The 'Young-old' and the 'Old-old'

Neugarten (1978) writes of an emerging age group in America which she calls the 'young-old'. She gives an age range of 55-75 for this group. The previous age demarcation line of 65 years corresponded with retirement, but in this country, as in America, retirement at 65 is no longer a hard and fast rule. We have seen in recent years a tendency towards earlier retirement. The banks and many local government and Civil Service departments already retire their staff at 60 years of age. Redundancies in our major industries and the number of 'golden bowlers' given out in the past 10 years has meant that we too are getting a younger retired population. There is even talk of an official lowering of the retirement age to 60 for men and 55 for women. All these social changes give credibility to Professor Neugarten's extra division of our life cycle; as she says, 'The young-old are distinguished from the middle-aged primarily by retirement and distinguished from the old-old by continued vigor and active social involvement'.

This is a new concept for us, but if we look at this age range as a definite age group we can see it has immediate potential. To begin with, individuals in this age group are likely to be better educated and to have a great deal more political elbow than we normally associate with the aged. This group have time, ability and enthusiasm to give in the voluntary field. There is a vast amount of aptitude, talent and capability just waiting to be harnessed for the benefit and service of the old-old. Above all, if their activity and vitality help to change the sterotype image of 'the old', that in itself will be a marvellous contribution to the aged.

In the community field the amount of work done for the old-old by the active retired is a magnificent indication of man's concern with and effective humanity towards his fellow men. Go to a 'meals on wheels' kitchen and see just who does the cooking; then look at the vast number of voluntary drivers who are going to deliver the meals and you will see a prime example of the young-old caring for the old-old. Look at local councils — in some areas almost totally dominated by the young-old age group. Citizens Advice Bureaux depend heavily on them as helpers for their compassionate listening ability, as do Marriage Guidance councils. In the hospital field they are often the ones pushing sweet and library trollies around, or guiding people through the intricate corridors to well concealed departments. Many children's wards are indebted to their voluntary granny figures for cuddles and tear wiping when mothers and fathers are not available. The young-old are indeed a valuable national asset.

Retirement

There are two ways of looking at retirement. The first is as a justly earned right to stop work, and to enjoy yourself doing the thousand and one things you've always wanted to do but never had time for. The second is as compulsory un-employment which makes people feel a loss of dignity, a loss of status, useless, financially deprived and with 20 years of unproductive life without a valued role to look forward to. This would presuppose that on retirement there is no useful function in relation to children, grandchildren, parents, spouse or extended family. It also supposes that the majority of people find no gainful employment after retirement: gainful that is either emotionally or financially. Finally, it supposes that there are a large number of people who have no life and nothing to offer outside their place of employment.

Exponents of this second attitude point to the pre-industrial societies in which the older person worked on at their craft or farm until they died, no doubt feeling very useful and productive. One reason for their activity was that few of them lived to the age of 65 anyway, and while the farmer may have continued to work his farm from choice as much as from necessity, his labourers probably did not have the same choice. It has been said that when Bismark first decreed that pensions would be paid at the age of 65, he knew it would not cause too great a strain on the budget because he did not expect too many of them to make it.

It is often suggested that retirement is fine for the professional classes because they can continue to work if they wish to but that the poor do not have the same privilege. What it really boils down to is that the rich can afford to retire but the poor cannot. Inherent, therefore, in any thinking on retirement is the fact that we must provide adequate pension rights to enable people to live without the fear of the stigma of 'charity'. Flexible retirement is something that could well be considered in this country, but more essential than anything else is the necessity to prepare people for what is, after all, a very large section of their life. We train young children to fit into our society; we train school children to man our industries and professions; we teach just about anything to anyone who cares to learn; so why don't we make a better job of teaching people how to live and enjoy their retirement years?

Retirement should be an uplifting new experience. We must teach people that the work ethic no longer need apply. They have done their share and now can relax and enjoy their interests, and if necessary find new interests, new hobbies, or expand old hobbies. Above all they have that most precious of all commodities, time. Time to give, time to keep to themselves, time to sit and think.

THE PLEASURE OF RETIREMENT

Yes, there is a hiatus when someone first retires. They wake at the same time to get to the factory or office. The habits of years take some time to shake off. There is a gap which seems difficult to fill, but over a period of time most people develop a different life-style. It may not be without trauma; adaptations must be made. There is usually a jockeying for position as there was when couples first got married; the 'who does what and when' scene all over again.

There is time to shop without rushing in and out between leaving the job and getting home to cook the evening meal.

There is time to take the dog for a walk and actually enjoy it, and time to invite friends for a meal. After a while people wonder how they ever had time to work. This world is a fascinating place and there are so many things to do and see, but not everyone recognises this fact. It is necessary to spend more time and money teaching the 'about to be retired' workforce that useful life does not end with retirement. Retirement is something they have earned; it is a right to be enjoyed. Boredom should have no place in retirement.

Hobbies can be profitable as well as enjoyable. A man whom I knew had a passion for auction sales and supplemented his retirement pension by buying at sales and re-selling either to shops or privately. This led to several antique dealers asking him to attend sales and bid for them on a commission basis. Another person whose hobby is soft toy making takes a stall in the local market occasionally and not only makes a profit but thoroughly enjoys the atmosphere and good-natured back-chat of the other stall holders. Yet another husband and wife team, both knitting enthusiasts, acquired a knitting machine and make pullovers to order for a local club, complete with the club emblem. Hobbies and creative activities are usually built up through the middle years of life so that by the time retirement comes along there is a pool of knowledge and expertise there to be expanded and enjoyed.

In the field of education too there is a fast growing realisation that older people wish to enhance their knowledge. Education, according to Morton Puner (1974), 'meets all the psychological and social needs of the older person'. He points out that in retirement a person may be designated an ex-person: an ex-nurse, an ex-postman, an ex-miner. Going back to school makes them a 'present student' — a new identity and a new role. Adult Education Courses can often be very well subscribed, whether they be arts and crafts, liberal studies, social sciences or courses about ageing itself. Older people also have a lot of knowledge to share. What could be more appropriate than a pre-retirement course including amongst its 'teachers' a retired person or two to relate and share their experiences.

Anything that gets older people away from the spectator

role (particularly non-stop television viewing) and back into participating, be it painting, writing, cooking, gardening, sports, hobbies or voluntary service schemes, can only be good. The role of spectator is so easy to adopt, but it is stultifying to the mind. ⋏

FINANCE IN RETIREMENT

It is important to look to the financial aspects of retirement well in advance. It is usual for the local office of the DHSS to contact people about 3-4 months before their 65th birthday (60 in the case of women) with the necessary claim form. It is obviously important to make sure that any entitled extras are included at this stage. Occupation pensions are also settled well in advance so there should be little difficulty in estimating what income will be available. Budgeting becomes more essential as the amount of money at one's disposal decreases. It is necessary to know how much will be left to live on and what, if anything, needs to be done to supplement it. Supplements may be in the form of part-time work, investments, annuities, or the application for a supplementary pension. If the amount of money coming in is not sufficient to live on, then the DHSS has the power to increase the pension by a supplementary pension. (See the subsection in chapter 3 entitled 'Claiming benefits'.)

Income from the state and occupational pensions, as well as income from investments and any earnings, are, of course, all subject to income tax. Some incomes are tax free, such as certain disablement pensions, pensions to war widows, pensions paid to holders of some gallantry awards and the Christmas bonus. There are also tax-free allowances to be off-set against the amount of tax payable. Apart from the individual allowance, these may include an age allowance, widow's bereavement allowance, blind person's allowance and child's service allowance. Nobody likes paying income tax at the best of times, but to pay more than one needs, especially in retirement, is folly indeed!

Conclusions

About half a million people retire from work every year (HMSO, 1981). It is one of the major changes that we make in our life-style, yet many of us enter it totally unprepared. The probability that many of the crises, insecurities and dilemmas of retirement could be averted by thoughtful preparation has resulted in an increase in the number of pre-retirement courses. Yet the availability of such courses is woefully inadequate. 'Only about six per cent of people approaching retirement receive any formal education' (HMSO, 1981).

The division of the retired into the 'young-old' and the 'old-old' may do something to allay the anxieties of those about to retire. If they can see the future as having another division after middle-age and before old-age, they may come to look at the years following retirement as the 'good years'.

The next generation of the young-old will be a very different type from those now old. They have lived in a time when social security has come to be seen as a right — not as a charity hand-out — and when trade unions have fought for, and won, shorter working weeks, so leisure is something with which they are already familiar. They are better educated and more socially and politically aware. They will expect, and demand, a higher standard of care. It is to be hoped that they will raise the science of geriatrics to a higher and more demanding level. Perhaps, in addition, they will see in voluntary work an outlet for some of their own free time, because voluntary work is good not only for the giver but also for the receiver and the community. More than anything else they may help to dispel some of the common misconceptions held about the aged and the process of ageing.

References

HMSO (1981). *Growing Older*, HMSO, London.
Luker, K. (1981). Elderly women's opinions about the benefits of health visitors' visits. *Nursing Times*, 77 (9) 33-35.

Neugarten, B. L. (1978) 'The rise of the young-old'. In *The New Old — Struggling for Decent Aging* (Ed. R. Gross, B. Gross and S. Seidman), Anchor Books, New York, 47-49.
Puner, M. (1974). *To the Good Long Life,* Macmillan Press, London.

Useful Publications

Allen, J. (1981). *Your Taxes and Savings in Retirement,* Age Concern, Bernard Sunley House, 60 Pitcairn Road, Mitcham, Surrey. Price 95p.
Your Rights — for Pensioners, Age Concern, Bernard Sunley House, 60 Pitcairn Road, Mitcham, Surrey, 1981. Price 50p.
Leaflet NP32: 'Your retirement pension'. Free from DHSS office.
'How to Pay Less Rates'. Free from local council offices.
Leaflet IR4: 'Income tax and pensioners'. Free from local tax offices.
Leaflet IR4A: 'Income tax and age allowance'. Free from local tax offices.

3 Myths and Reality

Most men when they think they are thinking are merely rearranging their prejudices

Knute Rocker (see Peter 1977)

Introduction

The majority of retired people live happy and fulfilled lives with their families and many of those who live alone also manage to find joy and pleasure in their old age. However, whatever the circumstances, retired people are all subjected to society's sterotyped image of 'being old'. Nearly all of us have preconceived ideas about most things, but probably no other section of the community is so vulnerable to being sterotyped as the ageing population. They are either sentimentalised as Darby and Joan couples or stigmatised as senile, decrepit or disabled.

Such predjudices can convince society that the elderly are incapable of change or of learning new skills, and many myths spring into being. For example the myth that most old people are deaf, so we have to shout at them; as for their sex life, well, that does not exist! It is a well known fact that all men are neutered at retirement and women don't do it after the menopause! If for some reason a man should escape castration at retirement and continues to enjoy his sexuality then he is a 'dirty old man', yet it's odd that we seldom say 'dirty old woman'.

It really is time that we exploded some of these very ridiculous myths and looked at elderly people as they *are*, not as we commonly *think* they are.

The aim of this chapter is to examine some of the myths and realities of old age. By gaining a more accurate perception of the elderly it will enable us to give better care to them.

What's in a Name?

A very popular misconception about the elderly is that you don't have to remember their name because they quite like being called 'Gran' or 'Grandpa'. The truth is that very few people like it, and they not only object to it, they seethe with resentment. Unfortunately, in a subservient position either in a hospital or home of one type or another, they tend to put up with it rather than lay themselves open to possible abuse.

Equally humiliating is the degrading and uninvited practice of calling elderly people by their Christian name. This is something that seems to be prevalent in nursing and rest homes where people tend to stay for long periods. If they were given reciprocal rights and were allowed to use the staff's Christian names, it might be quite a different story. One lady of 79 years gained the admiration and awed respect of the ward staff by replying in kind:

'Mrs Lily Brooks', said the ward sister to the consultant, handing him Mrs Brooks' notes.

'How are you today, Lily?' he asked, not even bothering to look at her, while thumbing through the notes. She turned to look at the card above her bed. In large letters it read: Mr George E . . . . . .

'Not too bad, George. How are you?' she replied.

Now that takes courage, and nobody ever called her Lily again.

When people are 'young middle-aged' and even when they are 'old middle-aged', they often do not object to being referred to as the 'old man' or 'old lady' by their children. When they actually become old they object very firmly to these titles. They no longer have the ring of affection that our children gave them, they now appear as insulting alternatives to their proper names. My own name was the first thing given to me by my parents. It was one of the first things I learnt. It proved that I was a separate person, I existed, I mattered. It was something which was my very own. My name, therefore, is important to me because it proves my identity.

When I grow old, if anyone other than my grandchildren,

call me Gran, I'll spit in their eye! The use of my Christian name will be restricted to those people whom I wish to use it. Outside that, its use will be rewarded by a sharp blast of disapproval and probably a wallop with my walking frame as well!

By not bothering to give the elderly the courtesy of using their proper title and surname, we reduce them to the status of children. No one has the right to diminish another person in this way.

The Darby and Joan Image

The image of the warm-hearted, loving and contented couple who wander hand in hand through the garden of love and continue to do so into the twilight years is very fine, but such couples are not too easy to find.

Most people stay together for 50 years or more because by the time they come to retirement they have got used to one another. Through affection and respect they have grown tolerant of each other's idiosyncrasies. The fact that he grunts when watching TV or that she sucks her teeth when knitting no longer grates on the nerves. He has grown accustomed to her face and she has got used to his ups, his downs, his smiles, his frowns. They pull together and work as a team and as 'a pair'. The passion of earlier years has grown into affection, warmth and the intimacy of shared joys and sorrows and family ties. Above all, a marriage that has lasted 50 years must be based on tact and diplomacy. As Morris Ernst so aptly put it, 'A sound marriage is not based on complete frankness, it is based on a sensible reticence' (see Peter, 1977).

There are, of course, extremes, and one occasionally comes across a couple who are bound together by hate.

"I knew one such couple who had been married for 47 years. There were no children to the marriage. The husband was a tall but meek man and the wife, although only five feet tall, was a strident voiced old harridan. She complained unendingly and bitterly of his faults, which usually consisted of not doing what she wanted, when she wanted, and on top of this her eyesight was deteriorating very rapidly. One of his morning jobs was to take her breakfast in bed and read the morning paper to her while she ate.

One night in his sleep, he died as quietly as he had lived, without fuss. It was their neighbour, who, hearing her banging about calling for him, went in and discovered the old lady shaking him, demanding that he get up at once. On being told that he was dead, she replied, 'He always was a selfish man. Who's going to read my newspaper for me now?' "

One wonders how such unions last, but they did and still do. Perhaps some people need to be submissive and others need to be dominant, and it may even be that they are happy in a miserable sort of way!

I have known other partnerships where the mutual hate came through in everything they did and said. I once asked a husband and wife who had been married for 51 years why they stayed together when they were both so obviously unhappy. She said, 'It was my money bought the house. I'll not move out and leave it to him,' and he said, 'I married the bitch. I'm stuck with her'.

If you look around your friends and relatives and take stock of their likes and dislikes, their pet hates and delights, their natural and acquired abilities, their submissive and dominant characteristics, you can safely assume that is what they will be like in retirement and old age. The characteristics may get a little exaggerated with time, but they will all be instantly recognisable. If their marriages are good and sound, they will weather the crisis of retirement and remain so. If they are rocking and unstable before retirement, then the loss of status and income is unlikely to improve them.

Sexual Activity in Later Life — There is Life After 70

> I pray that I may seem, though I die old, a foolish, passionate man
>
> W. B. Yeats (1935)

Of all the myths associated with ageing, none has such moral overtones as sexual activity. Sex is something the young think of as exclusively theirs, while the middle-aged decry its use by youth and shudder at its use by the elderly. The moralistic view is probably tied up with the old religious notion that sex was concerned with reproductive purposes only. It is, therefore, somehow considered immoral for older people to have sexual relations when there is no longer a reproductive function involved.

Today many people subscribe to the view that sex itself is an expression of love, affection and intimacy. With the advent of free and wholesale contraception to suit all needs, the reproductive function is no longer even a prime motive in sexual relations. However, in spite of this there still remains much bias against sex in ageing couples.

SOME FACTS

Sixty per cent of married couples remain sexually active into their mid and late 70s. Masters and Johnson (1970) say that the ageing male can be sexually active into his ninth decade and that, 'sexual interaction between older marital partners can be established easily, warmly and with dignity'. Kinsey, Pomeroy and Martin (1948) reported that male copulations averaged 4.8 per week for married males at 20 years to 1.8 per week by 50 years, 1.3 per week at 60 years of age and 0.9 per week at 70 years. So, on average, married couples of 70 years have sexual relations once a week.

Newman and Nichols (1960) studied 250 men and women between 60 and 93 years of age over a period of 7 years. They found that 54 per cent of married men and women were still enjoying their sex life. The number of sexual relations varied from three times a week to once every 2 months. They agreed with Masters and Johnson that people can be sexually active well into their 80s and 90s. Writing of the ageing female, Masters and Johnson (1970) say, 'There are only two basic needs for regularity of sexual expression in the 70-80 year old woman. These necessities are a reasonably good state of general health and an interested and interesting partner'.

NORMAL SEXUAL CHANGES IN AGEING

It is unfortunate that many men and women are not aware of the normal physiological changes that occur in the sex cycle with age. In the male that of slower erective response, a longer refractory period following orgasm, diminished force of the ejaculation and even the periodic loss of ejaculation is quite normal. In the female the greatest changes will be those of reduced hormone level, scanty vaginal secretion, and thining of the vaginal lining, all of which may cause inter-course to be painful, although all of this can be treated quite easily.

Because of ignorance, many men and women accept sexual dysfunction as a matter of normal ageing. As Masters and Johnson (1970) point out,

Tragically, yet understandably, tens of thousands of men have moved from effective sexual functioning to varying levels of secondary impotence as they age, because they did not understand the natural variants that physiological ageing impose on previously established patterns of sexual function.

Sexual difficulties are best discussed first by the elderly with their GP. It may be that a practical aid such as a cream to lubricate the vagina is all that is needed. If counselling is required, either marital or psycho-sexual, then the GP should know where the help is available.

PSYCHOLOGICAL FACTORS AFFECTING SEXUAL ACTIVITY

While physically there is a diminution in the sexual response in the elderly, it is not the physical changes that are usually the most damaging to continued sexual relationships. What inevitably spells the death knell for an elderly couple's sex life is the sad idea that it is not 'quite nice'. It is the attitudes of society and of their families and, most of all, their own ideas on sexuality which will tend to convince them that sex after a certain age is neither fitting nor seemly.

The fear of failure to perform sexually and the fear of ridicule are two of the most potent factors causing dysfunction, particularly in the male. There is no doubt that the most important sex organ is the brain — if you think you can't do it, then you won't. Jokes about sex are legendary, but those about elderly people and sex are especially ribald. They help to make the older couple feel degenerate or at best ludicrous. Why should the elderly, who have less time left than the rest of us, lose out in that most precious area, the warmth, love, comfort and intimacy of the sexual act. The fact that the vigour of youth has given way to the tenderness of age does not mean that sex is less enjoyable, less meaningful or less satisfying. In an age when communication is all important, sex, one could say, is the ultimate mode of communication between two people. The caring professions should always be willing to listen and advise on difficulties in the sexual field. If it is beyond our competence to advise the patient, we should refer them tactfully to the appropriate counselling service. Yet we are a long way from enlarging psycho-sexual counselling services to include the over 65s. There really does seem to be some truth in the suggestion that we de-sex people at 65 years of age irrespective of their sexual capacity or responsiveness.

THE 'DIRTY OLD MAN' SYNDROME

Most of us have been guilty of using this expression at one time or another. The 'flasher', the 'sex maniac', the 'sex deviant', the 'sex offender', are all labelled 'dirty old men'. But Kinsey, Pomeroy and Martin (1948) found that the majority of sex offenders were in their 20s and 30s — the average age was 35 years.

Morton Puner (1974) says:

> The incidence among the elderly of abnormal sex behaviour is low. And there are relatively far more dirty young men, to judge from the crime statistics, than there are dirty old men. The term itself, and that of 'old maid', are hardly defensible. All such sterotypes punish the old and are cruelly unfair. There are old men and women in varying degrees of physical and mental health and sexual adjustment, all with about the same needs for love and dignity.

DOUBLE STANDARDS

So many double standards are applied in our culture that it is not surprising that they appear in the field of sexuality. Why, for instance, is it quite appropriate for elderly women to hug and kiss babies and young children but not elderly men? Why do we look with favour on marriages between older men and younger women but not on those between older women and younger men. Yet the latter type of union would be more expedient in view of women's longer average life span.

A young 80 year old once gave me his interpretation of a happy retirement as 'Health, some wealth and sex on Saturday'.

Poverty and Ageing

Another strange misconception that society tends to hold about the older generation is that they don't need much money because they never go out. As long as they have enough to eat and are kept reasonably warm, they have nothing to complain about. Holidays, eating out and costly hobbies are all wasted on the old. They will be content with their knitting and their telly. Society gives them a pension that is never much above the poverty level and, at best, will be about a quarter of what the poorest of them would be earning prior to retirement.

Poverty, like many other things, is relative. What one person may look upon as extreme poverty, another may consider as relative riches and a starving inhabitant of the Third World might even think of as riches beyond their dreams or expectations. It would appear that many of the older generation do not feel actual poverty even when they are living below what we would consider the poverty line. The *Guide to the Social Services* (Family Welfare Association, 1981) says, 'The DHSS estimates that in 1976 580,000 families of people of pensionable age were entitled to but did not claim a supplementary pension'.

PRIDE IN OLD AGE

One reason for the poor take-up of supplementary pensions and grants is that many pensioners still consider them as charity: 'We have our pension, we are entitled to that, we paid into it, see, but we never asked for anything more than we are entitled to'. This is a hang-over from the pre-war days of Public Assistance and harsh means tests. Charity was something that was given to the deserving poor. You not only had to be poor and deserving but pretty deferential as well:

I remenber the Depression. You had to be very poor
before you got anything. I queued for hours for
some vouchers for free coal and it was awful. They
asked you so many questions about your private life.
You felt so humiliated. I would never do it again.

Another reason for the poor take-up is that there are so
many different types of benefit that few people know
what is, or is not, available or allowable. There are contri-
butory and non-contributory benefits. There are pensions,

allowances, 'special' allowances, grants, supplements and
rebates. It would take a veritable Houdini to negotiate a
way through the labyrinth: 'I did go to the office once to
ask about some heating because my friends told me I could
get some, but the people were so busy and they

gave me a lot of forms and I couldn't read them.'

Apart from the ordinary retirement pension, a person over 65 years (60 for a woman) may be involved with war pensions, supplementary benefit, a graduated pension, invalidity allowance, mobility allowance, rent rebate, rent allowance, rate rebate, industrial disability benefit and attendance allowance. In view of the intricacy of the system it is no wonder that the elderly person can be confused by it all. The rest of us certainly are.

CLAIMING BENEFITS

Our concept of poverty has changed dramatically since the turn of the century. People are no longer put into workhouses, although some might say that our modern equivalent, the 'rest home', is as bad. The poor are no longer expected almost to starve before they are allowed assistance or charity. Nevertheless, their income is drastically reduced at a time when they could and should be enjoying themselves. When they have the time and inclination, they don't have the resources.

Inflation can play havoc with their savings, the staff pension is no longer the prize they once thought it would be and the state retirement pension, known to most people as the old age pension, will not pay the weekly bills. Ask those old people who do claim supplementary pension where they get their clothes and most will tell you at jumble sales. Ask them when they last had their homes redecorated and they will probably have forgotten. Ask them if they are warm enough in the winter and be surprised that there are not more cases of hypothermia.

Anyone dealing with the elderly should always ask about their finances. There is no need to ask how much they have in the bank or what their income is, but they should be left in no doubt as to the reason for your interest. A straightforward general question, should prove sufficient such as 'How is the money situation? Do you have enough for food, heat and clothes? You do know that if you have less than £2000 in savings you might be entitled to a bigger pension?'

At least try gently to persuade those who do not claim

supplementary benefit but are entitled to it that the term 'charity' no longer applies. It is very difficult for most of us to be knowledgeable about all the DHSS allowances and grants, but supplementary pension and attendance allowance are two that we come into contact with quite frequently. Supplementary pension is a non-contributory benefit. At present it is payable to men over 65 and women over 60. The amount is worked out on a requirement less resources basis. The first £X net earnings of each adult in the household is ignored. A small amount of capital and income from it will also be ignored. On the assumption that if you never ask, you never get, a good reliable yard-stick is — if in doubt, apply.

A leaflet, which includes an application form, can be obtained at all post offices and DHSS offices. The elderly are seen in their own home by a visiting officer from the DHSS who will be as anxious as everyone else that those entitled to benefit should receive it.

The attendance allowance is payable to anyone over the age of 2 years who is either mentally or physically disabled and requiring constant attention. Medical conditions have normally to be satisfied for 6 months before the allowance is payable. The attendance allowance, which is tax free, is paid at two different rates: a higher rate, for those requiring attention by day and by night, and a lower rate, for those requiring attention either by day or by night. Forms are available at all DHSS offices and from most health visitors, social workers and district nurses.

Attitudes to the Elderly — The Right to Dignity and Respect

In reading about the ageing process it is astonishing how many authors look only on the negative and depressing side. They talk about the 'role-less role' of the elderly, of them having no vital function, of their diminished economic status and their lack of political power. As to physical ageing itself, an even more demoralising picture is painted. We are told that the skin becomes dry, hair gets white and sparse, joints stiffen, hearing and vision deteriorate, teeth fall out, and eventually incontinence and immobility prevail. Really you would think that the elderly should be grateful for the odd bout of pneumonia or the coronary to help them get away from it all!

It is a joy, therefore, to read about the work of people like Alex Comfort, who, in his book entitled *A Good Age,* is so positive in his attitudes to the whole field of gerontology. There is a great need for the Alex Comforts of this world to stand up and shout loud and clear on behalf of the older members of our society. 'We are not daft because we have passed a magic date-line. We have not lost all our intelligence because some idiot says our IQ starts to deteriorate at 26 years of age.'

The problem is that if you tell people something often enough, in time they come to believe it. Many young and middle-aged people believe that those over 70 are incapable of learning any new skill. However, age is no barrier to learning. It may take a little longer because the thought processes may be a little slower, but time is something the aged have plenty of. A life-time's experience helps the older person to see the short cuts to learning and therefore retirement can be the time for acquiring new skills.

Winston Churchill in his later life became a gifted painter. Many people in their 70s and 80s are gaining Open University degrees. One young widow of 72 years told me she had joined a car maintenance class because her husband had always seen to the car and she had not even known how to lift the bonnet up, much less recognise anything underneath:

'I had no idea, my dear, how fascinating the internal combustion engine could be. I'm getting very fond of my plugs and distributor, in fact I reckon I've got the cleanest plugs in the country.'

'What's the next step?' I asked, bewildered by all this new found technology.

'The advanced driving test and then I will take my grandsons, who are 14 and 16, to France for the summer holidays. They've promised to teach me disco dancing first.'

We all need to feel useful. As Peter Townsend (1957) points out, 'Elderly people lose their status when they lose the give and take of family life. From the social services they only take'. By allowing them to give again we return to them their dignity, their pride and their sense of purpose and that, after all, is what we would all like to end up with. The greatest disservice that society can do the elderly is to convince them that they can't do things simply because they have reached a certain age. There can be nothing more discouraging than the thought that society has decreed that you are old and therefore are no longer 'a doer'. It is to be hoped that the educational advances of the past few generations mean that the people retiring today will be better educated, more literate and more vocal than their predecessors. If the planners are right and we are going to see the projected increase in their numbers, then they should be able to make their voices heard at local and national level, because we cannot go on treating what will effectively be one-fifth of our population as expendable, obsolete and unimportant people.

What then *is* society's attitude to the older generation? Are they seen as geriatrics, as ill, frail, old, incapacitated people? Or are they thought of as 'chronic', whatever that expression may mean? Do most people really believe that 94 per cent of retired people live at home and that only 3 per cent of them are in hospitals of any kind? Is there a tendency to treat all older people in that indulgent but 'nurse knows best' way which is used on long-stay or continuing care wards?

"One 77 year old man told me that he had attended the out-patient department of a hospital where they had a blackboard on the wall with a supply of chalk to keep the children occupied while waiting. Sitting beside him was a rather fractious child and as he had always prided himself on his ability to draw — started incidentally when he worked for the Colonial Service, for which he had received a knighthood — he suggested to the child that they go and draw on the board. They had been drawing with great amusement and satisfaction for a few minutes when a young nurse passed by. She took my friend by the elbow and escorted him back to a chair, saying, 'The blackboard is only for the use of young children'. When he told the story he said she had placed the emphasis on the word 'young', thereby implying that although she recognised that he was a child, second childhood did not count."

There is an affinity between the very young and the old. Almost as if children recognise in the aged an unhurried calm — a willingness to listen to their flights of fancy. There is time without pressure and there is fun in going through the old stories and nursery rhymes. Many middle-aged people admit that they get more enjoyment and pleasure from their grandchildren than they ever did from their children.

The empathy between the generations could be exploited to both their advantages by extending the foster Granny and Grandad scheme in hospitals for children who, for one reason or another, do not get many visitors. There could also be a place for them in play groups and nursery set-ups to give the extra bit of loving to children from broken homes and those of single-parent families.

Alex Comfort (1976) describes a stereotype of the 'ideal aged person', and although he obviously has his tongue very firmly in cheek while writing, one cannot but wonder if there are still grains of embarrassing truth about it. He writes:

'Let us look at the stereotype of the ideal aged person as past folklore presents it. He or she is white-haired, in-active and unemployed, making no demands on anyone, least of all the family, docile with putting up with lone-liness, cons of every kind and boredom and able to live on a pittance. He or she, although not demented, which would be a nuisance to other people, is slightly deficient in intellect and tiresome to talk to, because folklore says that old people are weak in the head, asexual, because old people are incapable of sexual activity, and it is unseemly if they are not. He or she is unemployable, because old age is second childhood and everyone knows that the old make a mess of simple work. Some credit points can be gained by visiting or by being nice to a few of these sub-human individuals but most of them prefer their own company and the company of other aged unfortunates. Their main occupations are religion, grumbling, reminiscing and attending the funerals of friends. If sick, they need not, and should not, be actively treated and are best stored in institutions where they can be supervised by bossy matrons who keep them clean, silent and out of sight. A few, who are amusing or active, are kept by society as pets. The rest are displaying unpardonable bad manners by continuing to live and even on occasion by complaining of their treatment when society has declared them unpeople and their patriotic duty is to lie down and die.'

This passage may be amusing, but it is worrying to realise that there are many people who actually think like that. It is also important to question the assumption that not actively treating people of any age would be morally and ethically acceptable. There are some issues about caring for the elderly which we should all be worrying about, if for no other reason than that in the not too distant future a large number of us will have joined the ranks of the retired and will be on the receiving end of prejudice such as this.

At any age everyone has the right to respect from their fellow men. It is right to imprison people who physically abuse others, yet continuous mental abuse often goes un-recognised. Elderly people are often treated as if they are incapable of any thought, any ability or any power of reasoning: 'Just swallow these tablets; never mind what they are, they're good for you'. No one has the right to assume that sort of responsibility for another rational human being what ever their age. Nor has anyone the right to treat the elderly with less than common politeness or good manners.

"Not so long ago I saw what I first thought of as being a very kind gesture. A large car pulled up to allow an old dog to cross the road. The driver smiled benevolently as he watched the ancient animal hobble slowly and painfully across. Then a couple of elderly people tried to get in on the act, assuming, I suppose, that the same courtesy might be extended to them, they stepped off the curb to follow. The driver instantly pressed the horn and accelerated towards them, making the old couple jump back on the pavement. The old lady was shaken and distressed and the old man very angry that his wife should be treated in such a manner. We are well known as a country of animal lovers; what a pity we cannot extent it to include the older members of our own society!

The Need for Pressure Groups

If the retired population banded together and became active as a pressure group, then we might see a change in attitudes towards them. This is already happening in the USA, and what they do today we frequently do tomorrow, so there is hope. Perhaps a retired people's charter might help:

> We, the retired, having laboured long and hard, are now, by the nature of our efforts, entitled to respect for the knowledge and expertise which we have handed down. We claim the right to dignity because we have won that right through the indignity of a world war which we fought for freedom.
> We are people first and aged people second. We still have the same needs and the same values and we enjoy the same pleasures. We know there is an inevitable end to life, but we have no intention of sitting quietly in a corner waiting for it to happen. We will not be ignored, patronised, disposed of, or excluded, and we will fight to maintain our independence and individuality.

Conclusions

This chapter has examined some of the ways in which the elderly are stereotyped. It describes how an image of older people is often developed which is then related to *all* older people. Part and parcel of the stereotyped ideal older person is either the Darby and Joan couple or the toothless, deaf, senile, arthritic, shuffling old dear. If we think about their sexuality at all, it is briefly and easily dismissed. At a time when their dignity should be protected, they become nameless. When our turn comes, Heaven protect us from being called 'Gran' or 'Grandpa' by bright young things. We need to take our prejudices out and shake them about in the fresh air. If they are acknowledged and analysed, then it might be possible to rearrange them a little before putting them back into a compartment marked 'The aged — stereotype — prejudices relating to'.

As for poverty in old age, well the Bible tells us that Jesus said, 'The poor you have always with you' (*John* 12:8), and in fairness to them they always will be with us as long as the DHSS benefits are so complicated that few elderly people can understand them!

To enable older people to enjoy happy, dignified and satisfying lives we should be training them to maintain their independence. When they can no longer achieve independence and either they, or their family, look to society for help, that help should be given promptly, willingly and thoughtfully. The knowledge that help is available and forthcoming on request will sometimes be the deciding factor in whether an elderly person stays within their home environment or is admitted to 'care'.

References

Comfort, A. (1976). *A Good Life,* Crown Publications, New York.

Family Welfare Association (1981). *Guide to the Social Services,* Family Welfare Association, London.

Kinsey, A. C., Pomeroy, W. B. and Martin, C. E. (1948). *Sexual Behavior in the Human Male,* W. B. Saunders, Philadelphia.

Masters, W. H. and Johnson, V. E. (1970). *Human Sexual Inadequacy,* Little, Brown and Co., Boston.

Newman, G. and Nichols, C. R. (1960). Sexual activities and attitudes in older people. *Journal of the American Medical Association,* **173,** 33-35.

Peter, L. (1977). *Quotations for Our Time,* Methuen Paperbacks, London.

Puner, M. (1974). *To the Good Long Life,* Macmillan Press, London.

Townsend, P. (1957). *Family Life of Old People,* Routledge, London.

Yeats, W. B. (1935). 'A Prayer for Old Age'.

4 Dependency in Old Age

It should be the function of medicine to have people die young as
late as possible

E. L. Wynder (see Peter, 1977)

Introduction

For a small number of elderly people, infirmity causes dependence. This chapter looks at some of the ways in which
we, as professional workers, or caring families, can deal with
the problems caused by their infirmities. One answer is
residential accommodation or 'The Home'. While for some
elderly people going into a home is a relief, for most it is a
shattering and bewildering experience.

As well as having to cope with day to day living, many old
people also have to cope with a superfluous amount of
advice from relatives, friends, neighbours and professionals,
not all of which they either need or want. Trying to maintain independence in the face of vigorous opposition from
caring relatives can be a fearful task. Indeed when people
are ill and at their most defenceless and vulnerable, we often
add to their vulnerability by our polypharmacy! Most old
people have in their homes numerous bottles of drugs which
they have stopped taking — the majority of which they have
long forgotten why they started.

For many the effort of coping with their finances in the
face of exploding inflation is difficult in the extreme. They
simply cannot believe that something which cost 50p two
months ago, now costs 60p, particularly if someone is doing
their shopping for them. For some of us the moment will
arrive when we can no longer control our finances, when in
fact we can no longer count the pennies and make sense of
the answers. At that stage it will help if there is someone
around who cares enough to give assistance.

Dependence and Age

Dependence and inability to cope is not, of course, a matter of age. Some people are dependent at 60, while others are completely independent at 100.

Mrs Wright was a grand old lady who lived in sheltered accommodation where there was a warden on call, but the tenants looked after themselves, apart from the usual facilities of home helps and meals on wheels when necessary.

"Mrs Wright needed neither of these, nor any other external help, other than with shopping, a task happily taken over by her family. She did all the cooking and preparation for her 99th birthday. She repeated the performance the following year for her 100th birthday; this involved visits from the local mayor and mayoress and press photographer. On her 101st birthday her mince pies and cakes were better than ever, and the following year, on her 102nd birthday, she was the same upright, smiling, well dressed hostess, dispensing tea and sherry to all. A few months after her 102nd birthday she sent for her family, said she did not feel very well and died 3 days later, surrounded by the love and affection of three generations."

How early or how late in life we become incapable depends, as much on the luck of the draw, as on how clever we were in our choice of antecedents, or how well we looked after our health. Infirmity and incapacity may also be entirely different, especially when the dependent person is living with family or friends who do the actual caring.

"Mrs Harris lived with her son who worked as a road sweeper and a middle-aged niece who worked part time in a local laundry. By the time I met her she was already a local character and had spent the previous 10 years in bed and indeed went on to spend the next 2 years there until she eventually died aged 82. The initial reason for going to bed was a badly ulcerated leg, for which someone had suggested a period of bed rest. Who had suggested it was lost in antiquity, but by the time the community nurses were informed she was very firmly ensconced and, at 18 stone, was never to be dislodged. The house was a little two up, two down, terraced type without a front garden. Before

taking to her bed she had got her son to place it by the
window in the ground floor front room so that all she had to
do was open the window to talk to people walking by in the
street. After a few years in this position Mrs Harris knew all
the scandal and gossip of the neighbourhood and what she
didn't know she invented. The neighbours all used her to
pay their rent, clubs and insurance, leaving their books with
her. She could always be relied on to have stamps and change
and even the community nurses used her as a drop-off and
pick-up point. She once told me that the happiest years of
her life were those she had spent as infirm and bed-bound.
It was ironic that the legs never did heal, or it may be that
it would have been inconvenient for Mrs Harris if they had
done."

Problems Caused by Drugs and Medicines in Old Age

'A PILL FOR EVERY ILL'

Drugs and medicines can always cause problems, but nowhere is this more true than when caring for old people. Forgetfulness and frailty can provide a dangerous combination and the very fact of taking drugs can result in the elderly becoming more dependent.

Fortunately we are becoming increasingly aware of the dangers of modern pharmacology to the elderly. Drugs, which are normally safe, can in old age become extremely dangerous, due among other things to impaired renal excretion, slower metabolism and exaggerated side effects. The multiplicity of bottles found in some homes makes it doubtful whether they could possibly be taken in the prescribed doses, or at the prescribed times. We have only to look at the number of highly motivated young women who forget to take their contraceptive pill (which they only have to take once a day, and even that is marked out for them in calendar fashion). How much more difficult must it be for the elderly person, vision fading, hearing not so acute, to cope with up to 10 different medicines?

A report published a couple of years ago (Anon., 1980) stated that 'More than one in ten prescriptions dispensed in the UK have no instructions to patients on the container. "Use as instructed" presupposes a degree of comprehension many do not possess.' In the same article a recent Medico Pharmaceutical Forum speaker is reported as commenting, 'All patients are potential defaulters. Some people stop taking their medicines, like antibiotics, because they feel better, others because they feel worse.'

A further survey reported in the same article stated that

Patients failed to grasp the purpose of over half the drugs prescribed for them. They had not understood from 9 to 89% of prescription instructions and between 37 and 50% of patients had forgotten what the doctor told them, even if they had understood originally. Not all suppositories are for rectal conditions and one patient, because he didn't have piles, put his suppository up his nose.

Anyone concerned or involved with community health care can tell hair-raising tales of hoarding. Even though people do not want the drugs, do not understand why they have been prescribed, and have no intentions of taking them, they still keep them, just in case. Not only the elderly do it, we all do it. How many of us could put our hand on our heart and say we have not got any half-used bottles of medicines in the house. Add to that the very large number of proprietary medicines taken by the average member of the public, particularly the over-use of purgatives, and it is no wonder that our cupboards overflow.

The elderly person who goes to the GP with multiple problems may well come away with multiple remedies.

"A very elderly aunt wrote and told me that she had not been well and that her neighbour had sent for the GP. 'A very charming young girl', my Aunt said, had come and given her a lot of tablets to take at different times. The trouble was that she could not remember when to take them and because she was not taking them she felt very guilty about it all. On a follow-up visit, the charming young GP had impressed on her that it was important that she take them as they were for her heart, her blood pressure, her diabetes and her puffy ankles.

My Aunt was surprised and alarmed. She did not know there was anything wrong with her heart or her blood pressure, and wasn't diabetes a thing you died with? and her ankles had been puffy on and off for years. However, she determined to take the tablets properly and asked the GP to write the times and doses on a large sheet of paper. For 2 weeks she religiously took the tablets at the prescribed times, feeling worse every day. Eventually, remembering that before she saw the GP she had just not felt very well and now she felt dreadful, she took all the bottles to the loo and ceremoniously emptied them down the toilet. She reasoned that without the medication she was either going to die or get better and at 92 years of age, feeling as ill as she did, she said it really did not matter, in fact death was beginning to look like the more favourable of the two. Off she went to bed to await whichever event was destined to happen. Three days later she felt so much better that she realised her number had not yet been called."

The adverse effects of drugs may be due to an unintentional overdose because the elderly person has forgotten that he has already taken the drug. The overdose may also be due to a badly written instruction. An elderly man, who was reported to be 'falling about', showed me his eight bottles of drugs. Among them were two bottles of the same potent pain-killer. One was marked 'Take two for pain as necessary' and the other was marked 'Take two four hourly', which

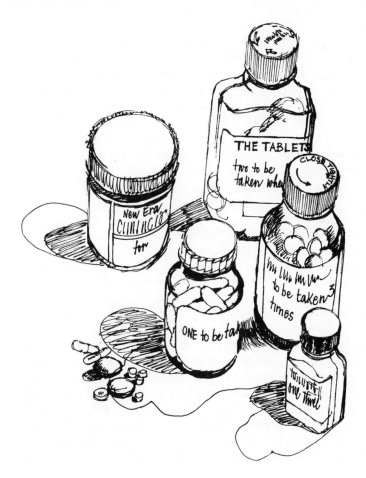

could easily have resulted in his taking a double dose of the drug — and this would certainly have made him fall about.

Childproof containers are very good at keeping little fingers out of trouble, but they are not without their problems. I am reminded of a lady who, completely out of character, suddenly became confused and incontinent. She lived in a sheltered housing flatlet and the warden reported her as wandering around at night trying to cook. She spent most of the day in bed, was incontinent, and seemed to be sleeping a lot. It had all started after the doctor's last visit. She had told him that she was not sleeping very well despite the mild sedative she took at night, so he had given her a stronger night sedative and at the same time had added a diuretic to get rid of the ankle oedema. The two bottles of tablets had duly arrived from the chemist in childproof and rheumatic finger-proof containers. She had promptly put them into two old screw-top aspirin bottles and then got them mixed up. So she took the night sedation in the morning and the diuretic at night. When the tablet she took at night did not help her sleep she increased the dose to two. The effect was dramatic. Fortunately, she returned to her normal state when all the tablets were removed.

REMINDERS ON WHEN TO TAKE DRUGS

Over the years I have tried many methods to get people to take their drugs at the right time. None of them have been completely successful because they all depend on the elderly person remembering what they are supposed to do and, if their main problem is remembering, then there is a difficulty straight away.

The best solution I have found is to buy a packet of envelopes and label them for the appropriate times of day; Monday 9 a.m., Monday 6 p.m., Monday night at bedtime, and so on. The prescribed medication is put into the envelopes and they are filed in a box in rotation. It can be done by a member of the family on their weekly visit, by a sensible neighbour or friend, or by the person himself if mentally alert. If the next envelope in line is marked Tuesday 9 a.m. and it is now Tuesday 11 a.m., then he at least knows that he has not had that dose. It has the added advantage that if the elderly person is going out for the day he need only take the appropriate envelopes with him.

Another system is to make out a chart, written in large clear writing, and to leave it wherever the drugs are kept. It is as well to find out what time people get up in the morning. There is little use in suggesting that they take the first dose at 7 a.m. if they don't normally get up until 9 a.m.

The Elderly and Their Financial Affairs

The elderly who find they can no longer cope with their financial transactions have few options open to them. They must choose the most trustworthy of their relations, friends or business advisors to act on their behalf. This can mean anything from giving the home help authority to draw their weekly pension to giving someone full legal powers of attorney. To give one's power of attorney to another necessitates being of sound mind and knowing what you are doing.

Those unfortunate enough not to be of sound mind may need to have their financial and legal affairs put into the care of the Court of Protection. This is an official body under the direct control of the Lord Chancellor. Application is made, usually by a member of the family or by a solicitor, to the Chief Clerk of the Court of Protection at Store Street, London. Even a proper power of attorney, given when the person was *compos mentis,* is no longer valid if the person becomes mentally incapable of knowing what is being done on their behalf. It may be that the elderly person owns vast estates and yet nobody can pay their bills because there is no authority to sign cheques on their behalf.

The Court will appoint a Receiver, who may be a relative, or failing the availability of a relative, then a solicitor or agent, to act for the person concerned. The Court of Protection exists, as its name implies, to protect the interests of people who can no longer do so for themselves. That applies particularly to the elderly mentally frail and mentally ill. The Receiver is normally empowered to pay the usual outgoings and bills on behalf of the protected person, but any major transactions, such as disposal of assets or investments or property, would need the permission of the Court. The incapacity of the person concerned needs to be verified by medical evidence and, in this case, it is usual for the GP to provide the necessary medical certificate.

Anyone who is concerned that an elderly person's financial affairs are being dealt with in a less than honourable way should contact their manager or supervisor and make sure that the appropriate private authorities are informed.

'WHAT'S THAT IN OLD MONEY?'

The vast majority of even the very elderly manage their money very well indeed, but just occasionally one still meets the person who has, for example, not yet mastered decimalisation and who still thinks in pounds, shillings and pence.

'Why don't you try meals on wheels, Mrs Heptel?' I implored one such lady who looked as if she had not had a square meal in months.

'Can't afford them,' she replied.

'But they're only 60p each and very good value for money.'

'How much is that in old money?' she asked.

'You can't go back to old money now, it just does not apply any more,' I argued.

'Yes, I know all that, but how much is it in old money?' she insisted.

'Twelve shillings, but . . . '. She stopped me in mid sentence.

'Twelve shillings each!' she gasped, 'I certainly can't afford that. It really is terrible how they make money out of us pensioners.'

She eventually decided to have meals on wheels, but every time she handed over the 60p to the volunteers who delivered them she reminded them that she was helping to run their cars.

Another elderly lady, who always called a 10p piece a florin, mystified a young boy scout by promising him a florin piece for weeding a patch of garden. He thought he was going to get a foreign piece!

The Need for Help

Dependency increases with disability, which in turn increases with age. The people, therefore, most likely to need help with their daily living requirements are those over 80 years of age, who live alone, probably on a restricted income, and who are possibly becoming mentally as well as physically frail.

For those of us who reach this stage it may mean that it is time for us to call upon our family for help. Whether they will be able, or willing, to give that help could well depend on the sort of relationship we have had with them in the past. The acting profession have a saying: 'Be nice to the people you meet on the way up, you might need them on the way down'. The love and affection we show to our relations when they are young and dependent could well be what is returned to us when we are old and dependent on them.

"The four Pearson sisters never married but they all adored — and whenever they could, spoilt — their three brothers' children. The children grew up knowing that 'the aunts' could always be counted on to take their parts and fight their battles. Lucy worked as a housekeeper and often had the nephews and nieces for holidays. Florence lived in a little rented flat by the sea and worked as a typist. She too enjoyed seeing the youngsters at weekends and holidays. Mary worked in a bank and had rooms in London; she could always be relied on for overnight stays and Christmas pantomimes. Anne had been in service as a cook. All her holidays had been spent with one or other of the brothers; she had taught all the nieces and the nephews to cook and appreciate good food.

When the time came for them to retire, one of the nephews bought a house and offered it to them at a nominal rent. The four of them lived together, pooling their resources, happy amid photographs of the family, their various weddings and subsequent births, ever ready to fly to the rescue of any member who needed them.

As they became older and frailer the system worked in reverse. Now it' was the turn of the nephews, nieces, great-nephews and great-nieces to show their appreciation, and they did so willingly and gladly. One by one infirmity and death claimed the old aunts, but they all died at home supported by their family."

It is better to bank benevolence than money; love and empathy carry a higher interest rate than stocks and shares.

FRIENDS AND FAMILY

Relatives come in many sizes, shapes and forms. They also differ in the degree of constructive or destructive advice and criticism which they offer to the elderly relative and/or friends, neighbours and other carers. They include those who care daily for their infirm, dependent elderly, doing an heroic job; often not seeing it as anything at all out of the ordinary; accepting that it is their duty, even privilege, to do so. The trouble is that we sometimes leave the burden with them too long for them to cope alone. If only we can recognise the strain before it becomes too great. If only we can give them the necessary support when they need it so that they can continue to do the job. The magic words are, 'when they need it', not next month, or even next week, but when they need it, and if that means 'today' then that's when they should have it.

When we talk of relatives we must realise that friends sometimes take on the duties and burdens of family and do so admirably. There are many people who get on better with their friends than with their own family. Families, after all, are wished on us; friends we choose ourselves. A colleague once told me that he got on very well with all his family because the nearest one was a hundred miles away and, as long as he saw them about once a year, they remained great friends.

There are also many families whose members, although they do not live with their elderly relatives, keep a close and loving contact by frequent visits and telephone calls.

At the other end of the spectrum, there is another type of relative, well known to all health and social service departments. They are known by many names but probably the most polite is 'the visiting relative'.

THE VISITING RELATIVE SYNDROME

This syndrome develops from a set of circumstances, but to begin with you need a relative who does not visit very often. General practitioners would probably say that the visiting relative syndrome only occurs at weekends, and that it always coincides with their Sunday or bank holiday lunch! But this is not strictly true, and it can happen on any day of the week.

Although this syndrome has many manifestations, there are some symptoms common to all attacks. First, there is the descent, often without warning, of the relative. Secondly, there are loud exclamations at the accumulation of non-essential items, such as the previous year's newspapers. Thirdly, there is the demand to see the GP or whoever, who is then informed that mother/aunt/gran can no longer cope and cannot possibly be left alone for a moment longer. The usual phrases are trotted out: 'Something must be done' and 'They'd be far better off in a home'. Having performed what they consider to be their duty, they return from whence they came, feeling righteous. When the object of their attention receives the inevitable visit from the GP, health visitor, social worker or district nurse, they are usually very grateful that the hurricane has passed for another while and that they can settle down to doing their own thing again.

Another manifestation of this odd syndrome is the follow-up telephone call to one or other of the statutory services, or even to the GP if they did not manage to get him away from his Sunday or bank holiday lunch. It can be a belligerent demand, such as, 'What are you going to do about my mother/aunt/gran?' or a long sad explanation of how they would love to have her but . . . . These long explanations can end up with a request for a visit, such as, 'She really should be in a home but please don't tell her I asked you to visit.'

On one such follow-up visit, the door was opened to me before I could even knock and I was in the house and sitting down before I even said who I was.

'Yes, yes, dear, I've been expecting you. It's my niece isn't it? It's always the same after she visits. When she is here she goes on and on, and it is easier to agree with her. So when she said I would be better off in a home, I said, "Yes".'

'But you have no intention of going anywhere, have you?'
I asked.

'No, of course not. I have Mrs Edwards from next door. She
comes in most days and Doris my home help is wonderful
and the boys from the local church do my garden. I manage
very well.'

'How often does your niece visit?' I asked, wondering
really when we could expect the next visitation.

'Not very often,' she replied with an impish grin. 'She's
a kind girl really, she means it for the best.'

And of course generally speaking they *do* mean it for the
best. It is easy for us to get exasperated with them because
they seem to do little except visit, disturb the *status quo* and
then vanish. But they do have a use because they make us
look again at a situation. Maybe we have become complacent;
perhaps the elderly person is at risk if left alone and they
might just have a point in telling us to get on with doing
something constructive.

THE WIDER COMMUNITY

Although family is something we all tend to take for granted,
there will always be a percentage of the population who
have no immediate family. People who are now in their 80s
and 90s have lived through two world wars. The first killed
many of their brothers and lovers and the second their sons
and husbands. They have outlived most of their own generation and if there is the odd sister or cousin still alive they
will be equally frail and equally elderly.

Many people in this situation have, however, got good
links with the wider community, with neighbours, local
churches, the milkman, the postman, voluntary visitors,
home helps, local clubs, both luncheon and recreation, the
statutory organisations such as the Primary Health Care Team
and the Social Services Department. In many areas most of
the services are highly organised and freely available. The
trouble is that the newly retired do not know where they
are.

They'd Be Far Better Off in a Home

Eventually, despite family care, regardless of the amount of community support, and notwithstanding the state of our finances, a small proportion of us — three in every hundred — will end up in a hospital of some sort. Of that three, one will be in a general hospital, one in a geriatric hospital and one in a psychiatric hospital.

Another three in every hundred will end up in residential accommodation of some sort; that is, they will voluntarily go into, or be put into, or be forced by circumstances into 'a home'.

Isn't it amazing how many people say of others, 'He/she would be far better off in a home', and isn't it equally amazing that they should think the mere fact of expressing such an opinion should be enough to make the authorities jump in and do it? But what is frightening is the number of educated, responsible members of the medical, nursing and other caring professions who say and think the same thing. Fortunately, an Englishman's home is still his castle and there are very few occasions when he can be dislodged from it.

The 3 per cent of the elderly who live in homes include those who live as permanent residents in hotels, guest houses and private nursing homes. They account for about 1 per cent; the other 2 per cent will be those who live in either Social Service Part III accommodation (so called because it was Part III of the National Assistance Act 1948 which placed the responsibility for providing care for the elderly homeless on the social services departments) or they will live in privately run registered rest homes, or in homes run by the various charity/voluntary organisations.

There are, as we all know, homes and homes. They range from the fabulous to the degrading. They can be warm, human, cheerful places at one end of the spectrum; at the other end they can be unbelievably sad and debasing. The same home can mean different things to different people, depending on how gregarious or how private a person you happen to be. It can mean something one chooses to enter of one's own free will, or a place in which you were put. It can be a combination of home and residential club or solitary confinement in one room for the rest of your natural, or

DIFFERENT TYPES OF HOME

The homes run by the social services departments, known to the general public by various names, such as welfare homes or old folk's homes, and unfortunately still feared by some old people as being akin to the workhouse, are, on the whole, well run and maintained. Unfortunately, because of the number of very frail and dependent elderly admitted to the social services homes, and the number always awaiting admission from hospital or community care, it is unlikely that people will ever have the choice of entry just because they no longer wish to live alone.

There is always a difficulty in deciding at what stage an elderly, dependent, frail person is no longer suitable for a Part III home and now needs geriatric attention, particularly if the geriatric beds are in short supply. Paradoxically, those patients who have been rehabilitated on geriatrics wards and are considered suitable for Part III may have to wait a long time because the homes are full. Suitability must take second place to availability. Certainly, bargaining goes on in many health districts, involving a lot of 'You take one of ours and we'll take one of yours'. A sad situation for the old, to be placed here or there without choice and without consultation. They may be admitted from one home and be discharged to another. One solution might be the district health authorities running their own nursing homes, or using more contractual beds in existing private homes.

The next, and perhaps the best, choice of residential accommodation is within the voluntary or charitable organisations. The churches, the professions, the trade unions, the armed forces, the masons, you name it, they probably have a home somewhere or other. The standards are high, the waiting lists usually long, and the criteria for entrance fairly strict. For instance, many of them have an upper age limit of 80 and some of them are terrified by illness of any sort. One home, run by an excellent church organisation, refused a lady who had been on their waiting list for 2 years; she was on the point of acceptance when she had to have a pacemaker fitted. They would have nothing to do with her despite being assured that she was fitter and more active than she had been for years.

Another difficulty is that any home is only as good as its staff on any day of the year. It would seem that there is a particular breed of people who opt to become matrons, wardens, housekeepers, directors, or what have you, of residential homes. If they stay for long, many of them become bossy, domineering, intimidating and peremptory. At the other extreme there can be frequent changes of staff, with an endless change of faces and no continuity of care.

However, the voluntary and charitable homes are usually very safe places, because there is an interest taken by the parent body and normally a fairly generous supply of money available from the benevolent funds. They have committees whose members visit and talk to the residents and if the person in charge gets too intolerable then the committee can ease them out.

But what happens if you want or need this sort of accommodation and you did not belong to any profession, and your father was not a mason, and you were not a member of the armed forces or a trade union, and you have no call on a particular church? Now you enter a different league, the world of the private rest home. This is where you could do with either a crystal ball or intimate knowledge, to guide you through the jungle, because this is where the good is very good and the bad is awful. I am always slightly suspicious of any home that has rows of geriatric chairs around the walls; it implies unbending rules and destructive inactivity. I always suggest to any elderly person who is contemplating going into a home to book in for a month first of all, before they commit themselves to it for life.

There are many people who go voluntarily, indeed eagerly, into homes. People with a strong religious or professional bias often feel happier among their own. Then there are the amiable, easy-going, sociable people who enjoy communal living, and rather than live alone, they prefer to live in a residential community. But, there is little doubt that the vast majority of people in 'homes' of one sort or another are there because of necessity and not choice; that does not mean, of course, that they are all unhappy.

Mrs. Martin

Some homes are excellent. In these, residents can live as independent a life as they like. In America such places are often referred to as 'residential clubs', where they provide the best facilities while meeting the special needs of their elderly clients. However, at the sad, bad and terrible end of the scale there is a grey area housing, generally speaking, the senile and very frail who cannot shout about the indignity and uncompassionate environment in which they have to live. Some of them would make the old workhouse seem like a rest cure; many of them are unregistered because they contain only three, or less, elderly people. These are the ones we should all shout about when we find them. If ever we enter a home and think, 'I should hate to end up here', then we should do something about it. For the unfortunate people living there, there is no reprieve from their life sentence other than death.

If anyone is wondering who to shout to, it is the duty of local authorities' social service departments to inspect registered rest homes, and it is the duty of the district health authority to inspect registered nursing homes.

HOW TO WORK THE SYSTEM

There is little to help those who wish to enter a home, or want to help a relative choose a home but don't know where to start. At the top end of the scale are the small flats or one-roomed flatlets which the retired people furnish themselves, and in which they are responsible for their own welfare but there is a warden on call if needed. This type of 'sheltered accommodation' is available in both the private and the public sectors. Most housing authorities will willingly transfer council tenants from three-bedroomed council houses to flatlets if they can. Housing departments also have lists of all housing associations with property in their area and will supply lists on request. (See Appendix 2 at the end of book.)

If a little more supervision is necessary, then organisations such as the Abbeyfield have homes in which the tenants again furnish their own rooms and are responsible for them, although main meals are provided. Most of the housing associations have an age limit and are also quick to point out that they cannot provide care other than in an emergency.

For those who are looking for full residential care, the first thing to look for is some connection with one of the voluntary or charitable organisations. The major churches, professions, ex-servicemen's associations and trade unions all either run homes or have connections with particular homes. Ask the local social services department for a list of the registered homes in the area; ask at the library for a copy of the *Charities Digest,* which contains the national addresses of all the charities and voluntary organisations. Pester the vicar, priest, minister or rabbi. Pester the health visitor, social worker and GP. Visit the local Citizens Advice Bureau. Ask and keep on asking until you have all the knowledge necessary to make a rational, practical decision. If you annoy people enough they will come up with the answers — if only to stop you annoying them.

There will of course be many people who have no affiliations with any organisations, or even if they do have a claim on a particular home, do not wish to go there, or who would like to go but cannot wait until Nature creates the vacancy. A very charming nun once put it admirably when I enquired as to the possibility of a vacancy: 'We are waiting,' she said, 'for God to call.' For the elderly who cannot maintain themselves in their home or wait for God to call, the social services department has a statutory duty to provide!

LOCAL AUTHORITY HOMES

These are administered by the social services departments and house about 131 000 people throughout the UK at any one time. The average age of admission is about 82 years and 'increasing number of residents are mentally infirm or have physical disabilities, or both' (HMSO, 1981). Provision will probably always be below the need, but referral is direct to the local social services department, and even if they do not have a vacancy they do have a lot of expert advice to offer.

THE PRIVATE SECTOR

To enlarge on the private sector one needs local knowledge. Some rest homes provide more care than others; in some there is round the clock attention and some of the staff have a genuine liking and respect for elderly people. Others see it as a quick way of making money, with little regard to the personal dignity of those they live off. The important thing is that someone from outside, whether family or a friend, maintains contact and is seen to be vigilant in the elderly person's interest.

NURSING HOMES

The majority of nursing homes are privately administered and, apart from some very specialised ones like the hospices, are divided into surgical and non-surgical. While some of the surgical homes will take medical patients; those without operating facilities will probably contain a large percentage of chronic sick, mentally and physically disabled, elderly people.

The private nursing homes range in elegance from those with private suites to a room containing four beds, four commodes, and four very senile incontinent old people. The fees will be equally divergent, but they will always be more than rest homes because the nursing home must, by law, have trained nursing staff in attendance, day and night. The amount of care needed will also demand a higher ratio of staff to number of clients/patients than will be found in rest homes. As far as choice goes, in common with most things in this world, 'You gets what you pays for'.

Many elderly people are put into nursing homes for long term care because the families feel it would be better, or nicer, than being in a 'geriatric' ward. Some are put there because members of the family mistakenly believe, or are led to believe, that there are no hospital beds available. Before taking on such a heavy financial burden, families would do well to explore the situation, and if necessary demand that hospital provision be made.

WHO PAYS?

Residential care, be it in the public or private sector, costs a great deal of money. Within the public sector, local authorities are required by law to charge residents for accommodation. This could mean anything from charging the full economic rate, if the person can afford it, to accepting clients with just their state retirement pension. Pensioners entering a social service department home would forfeit their pension and be entitled only to pocket money.

Many of the voluntary homes are subsidised by the parent charity; nevertheless, residents will be required to pay, and this could well be on a sliding scale according to means. The amount varies with each home; some are willing to accept residents for their pension plus what can be added by the DHSS.

The realm of the private nursing home is a very expensive one. The larger, nationally known nursing homes and private hospitals are patronized by the very wealthy or by those of the 3½ million individuals who are members of a private health insurance scheme. Within the middle range are thousands of small establishments, some surgical, some medical, some both, where you still need to be fairly affluent or privately insured if you are going to avail your-self of their services. At the bottom end of the scale are the small medical nursing homes — the type that abounds on the south coast — in which the cost is more likely to be determined by the size of the room. A single ground floor room may be twice the price of a shared room in an attic. In the summer, when there could well be several empty rooms, fees might even be negotiable.

All private rest and nursing homes are run as businesses and, as with any business, if you receive a service you must expect to pay for it. The person who pays in this business is the client/patient or the person who requests the service on their behalf. If you pop auntie into a nursing home and 3 weeks and a £600 unpaid bill later you find that auntie either can't or won't pay up, you might just find that you are required to pay the bill yourself.

"When I was very new to the community game and rushed around giving everyone the benefit of my inexperience, I was asked one day by a neighbour to visit a Mrs Younkin and advise her about nursing homes as she wished to go to one for a few weeks. It was a very twee house. Plastic gnomes fished from a plastic fishing pond and others sat around on toad-stools, looking bewildered at the collection of sea shells and imitation flowers planted in the garden. The front door and windows were painted purple with the edges picked out in lime green. Inside, the walls, shelves, and all available surfaces were covered in knick-knacks. The neighbour took me up-stairs to meet Mrs Younkin. In a shocking pink nightie and a green bedjacket, she looked a bit like one of her gnomes.

'I have a virus infection and need a lot of attention,' she informed me, 'I think I'd better go into a nursing home for a few weeks. Poor Miss Butcher, ' indicating her neighbour, 'has been so kind, so good, but I can't trade on her good nature any longer.' There were some clucking noises from Miss Butcher which indicated that she too agreed with the decision.

In my ignorance I missed the non-verbal messages that were flying around, but, in fairness, what I did not know at that stage was that Mrs Younkin frequently took herself to bed for a rest and Miss Butcher had always looked after her.

At some stage of the 'illness' she would go through the formula of telling Miss Butcher how grateful she was, but she really could not expect Miss Butcher to spend all her time 'looking after silly little me', and that she really must go into a nursing home, to which Miss Butcher, in the past, had always replied, 'That's all right, I don't mind, you just get better.' Now suddenly Miss Butcher had decided that she had had enough of Mrs Younkin so she had taken her up on the nursing home remark and sent for me!

With speed and efficiency that delighted Miss Butcher I discovered a local nursing home that had a vacancy and was prepared to take her at once. Two days later, furious at what she considered lack of doting attention, poor food, high fees and an old lady in the next room who thought her room was the toilet, she packed her bag and went home. The nursing home owner was not amused and there were vague suggestions that if they could not get the money out of her they might be looking in my direction. Fortunately, Miss Butcher was a witness that I had only carried out Mrs Younkin's request and I learned a very valuable lesson in economics."

Assisting people into rest or nursing homes is really a job for the family. They may be glad of advice and help but the responsibility is essentially theirs. Professional staff should only become involved when there is no family or they are unable or unwilling to help. If friends and neighbours feel that sometimes the professional worker is playing the Devil's advocate by pointing out all the difficulties, it is probably due to long experience of the dilemmas that can arise, not least of which is the frequent change of heart that many elderly people have when it comes to leaving their homes.

HELP WITH FEES

The DHSS will help those people on Supplementary Benefit and who need rest/nursing home accommodation. The amount payable will cover the cost of social services department homes, many of the voluntary homes and some sharing rooms in some of the private homes. It would not cover private nursing home care even at the lowest end of the scale. Attendance Allowance may also be granted and is always worth applying for. Added to the DHSS allowance and with a bit of help from the charities it might even tip the balance for the rest of nursing home fees.

Charity funds are available from many sources, and it may be worth spending a little time consulting the *Charities Digest*. Some charities will give a weekly allowance, whereas others give a grant towards a certain project.

Annuities are another way of increasing your income during your lifetime. By paying over a lump sum to an insurance company, they will contract to pay you a certain amount annually for life. The amount will depend on what you invest, on how old you are and your sex. Women live longer than men and so can expect less of an annual return on the assumption that they will draw it longer. One thing to point out to anyone thinking of an annuity is that once the contract is made, the capital sum is not recoverable.

Conclusions

Those of us who live into ripe old age stand a bigger chance of becoming dependent. There is no doubt that the elderly, dependent infirm are at risk — as much from society's good intentions as from its bad ones. Well intentioned relatives can be as destructive as well intentioned doctors with their high-powered drugs. When an independent life is no longer possible, we sometimes place them at considerable risk by putting them into badly run homes.

If we fail to recognise the build-up of intolerable stress situations between the elderly and those caring for them, we add to the vulnerability of the elderly person and increase the risk of them suffering verbal, if not physical violence. Most elderly dependent people are cared for by their families with great devotion. Whether the devotion is due to love, loyalty, respect or conscience may not be of great consequence. What does matter is that we recognise it, support it and give the appropriate help where and when needed.

References

Anon. (1980). Editorial. *World Medicine,* July issue.
Charities Digest, Family Welfare Association, London (published annually).
HMSO (1981). *Growing Older,* HMSO, London.
Peter, L. (1977). *Quotations for Our Time.* Methuen Paperbacks, London.

5 Some Special Problems of Later Life

To be old and helpless is unfortunate. To be old, helpless and alone is heartbreaking

(Taken from this chapter)

Introduction

The problems faced by elderly people which are discussed in this chapter have social as well as medical connotations. They include such handicaps as incontinence, alcoholism, isolation, loneliness, hypothermia and the new social disease of mugging. They are not so much age-related as age-enhanced because although they are found in all age groups and in all social classes they have a more profound effect on the elderly. These conditions tend also to be related to each other in that an isolated, lonely person may take to the bottle as a means of oblivion, and this in turn can lead to falls and hypothermia, or to increased incontinence.

The focus of this chapter is an attempt to identify and alleviate the causes of these problems. These are all conditions which can be helped, some treated, some cured, and some alleviated. All that is needed is a commitment from the caring professions, a commitment of time, patience, tact and common sense.

Incontinence and the Elderly

According to the blurb issued by one of the manufacturers of incontinence pads, there are 17 000 000 individuals in the UK suffering from this particular indignity, and there is little doubt that the majority of them will be in the upper age range. Forty per cent of older women are said to have some degree of loss of urinary control (Hood, 1980). So if there are so many of us suffering from it, why is it that in our

society incontinence has become synonymous with guilt and shame and rejection?

Incontinence is, after all, only a symptom of a disease, and in the case of the elderly this particular symptom is as likely to be social as it is medical. It can be that the home conditions are so poor that they are not conducive to a good toilet regime. The toilet may be too far away for them to get there in time, or the corridor so cold that the older person waits too long rather than face the winter chill.

It is now well recognised that a significant proportion of incontinence in elderly people is due to their decreased mobility which prevents them from reaching toilet facilities in time, and this is a matter which surely must be within the power of the caring professions to do something about. We are indoctrinated from a very early age to believe that there are only two places for urine, the bladder or the lavatory pan — and incontinence has been described as the race between the two! The only category of person allowed to urinate with impunity is, of course, the very young infant, but even they are constantly encouraged to think of dry as beautiful. Young mothers vie with each other on the toilet training issue and children who are late developers in this field are a great disappointment to their parents.

So it is not to be wondered at that we grow up with such an ingrained horror of 'wetting' ourselves. For the elderly, the problem of incontinence is an ever present worry. There are few older people who do not have some cause for concern at some time in their lives. The winter cough, the run for the bus, even the hearty laugh can bring with it the fear of dribbling stress incontinence. The age of the oral diuretic has done its share too. The oedema is no longer in the legs, for the slow-moving arthritic or otherwise disabled person it is sometimes, unfortunately, on the carpet all around the legs.

Old people go to great lengths to hide the 'shame' of incontinence. They will deny its existence even in the face of overpowering nasal evidence. Urine, when fresh, may smell like new mown hay, but after a while it takes on an equally distinctive, if less delightful fragrance.

I sometimes wonder if the conspiracy of silence and embarrassment involved with incontinence is not growing in proportion to the growth of the cosmetic industry. They are fast turning us into an odour-free race. We are not even allowed to sweat any more: we must plug up our sweat glands with deodorants and antiperspirants. We are socially unacceptable if we smell of anything other than their latest perfume, mouth-wash, aftershave, and so on. It is to their advantage to make us aware and ashamed of any natural body odour, so that they can then sell us some outrageously expensive preparation to help us get rid of it.

For the elderly, one of the most important social criteria

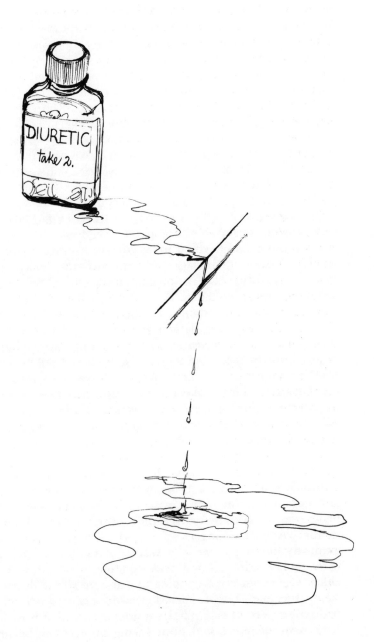

in our smell-free society is that they be continent. Indeed, incontinence is the main excluding factor for those people applying for sheltered and Part III accommodation, while private rest homes and guest houses quickly complain if any of their residents become incontinent. It is therefore most important for those who care for the elderly to give them particular help in this area. We need first of all to convince the elderly that they are not alone with their problem, that most people have trouble at some time or another, and that it is not shameful or illegal or immoral. We need to convince the families and friends of the elderly that all incontinence is treatable, that it is only a symptom of a disease, and that the disease, once diagnosed, may even be curable.

"I was once asked by a neighbour to visit a lady who, she said, was no longer able to cope. The address was one of the older terraced properties, in a sad state of disrepair. The whole place looked neglected, uncared for, unloved and unwanted; a bit like its owner and her cat. She was 78 years old and it looked as if it could have been 100. Both she and the cat also looked unwashed and undernourished.

There was a young woman with her when I arrived. This turned out to be a visiting niece; visiting, as she quickly pointed out to me, from a great distance and unlikely to be back again for a long time. When I introduced myself the niece insisted that I take the chair she had been sitting on by Auntie's bed because Auntie was deaf and would not be able to hear me if I sat anywhere else. It seemed a very sensible arrangement, so I sat down.

The old lady had a deaf aid which she refused to use. She admitted tearfully to being lonely, isolated and depressed. She didn't want to leave her home but did not want to be left alone in it. She didn't want to lie in bed all day but saw no reason for getting up. She didn't bother to cook but had in the past refused meals on wheels. While I talked to her I gradually became aware of a feeling of dampness penetrating through my skirt. I knew it wasn't me, so it had to be the chair. The room was beginning to warm up and with the heat came the inescapable malodour of stale urine and the realisation that when I left I would take some of it with me. Although the niece had been sitting in the same chair she had a guaranteed immunity in the shape of a plastic raincoat. Obviously previous experience had taught her that discretion was the better part of valour as far as sitting down in her aunt's house was concerned."

The moral of the story is be careful where you sit and the sadness of it was that her incontinence and self-neglect was all due to isolation and depression. The old lady improved with rehabilitation by the geriatric department, day care by the social services department, by the introduction of the home help and meals on wheels services and the involvement of the local church visiting group. Someone cared again. There was a reason to get out of bed in the morning — she had to let the home help in or get ready for the day centre. Even the niece invited her for a holiday when there was no longer any danger of her wetting the chairs.

Dealing with incontinence requires a lot of tact, sympathy and good plain practicability. Many elderly people will deny that they have any difficulty and some of them will deny it very strenuously. We have many years of conditioning to break through before it will be accepted that the inability to contain one's urine in one's bladder is not shameful. Treatment must be positive, there is no place for the quick visit by a GP or community nurse and donation of incontinence pads. Surely we owe it to our clients or relatives to first of all find out *why* they are incontinent.

A mid-stream specimen of urine will prove the presence, or not, of bladder infection. Rectal impaction can also cause obstructive disorders of micturition; in this case the bowel can be cleared and re-educated. Urinalysis will detect the possibility of diabetes. Accurate history taking and the keeping of a record chart over a period of a week will give invaluable information. Stress incontinence caused by weakness of the bladder outlet due to stretching by the pelvic diaphragm can be helped by pelvic exercises or by surgical repair. The uninhibited neurogenic bladder and the unstable bladder have very similar patterns. As the bladder fills uninhibited contractions develop and the awareness that the bladder needs emptying is followed quickly by a feeling of urgency and within seconds by the actual emptying of the bladder. These conditions can be helped by the use of certain drugs which inhibit the impulses causing the contractions and by getting the person concerned to follow a bladder routine. What they must do is develop a bladder habit. With the aid of a timer, be it an alarm clock or kitchen timer, they are reminded to go to the toilet every 2 hours. It may be possible for the interval to be increased as bladder retraining takes place, but even if it cannot a visit to the toilet every 2 hours is worth the joy of dry pants and odour-free clothes.

The most important part of treating incontinence is the attitude of the person doing the treating. If that person will go to the bother — and it is a lot of bother — to explain to people how their bladder works, why they are incontinent, how the treatment will work, how long it is likely to take and the importance of record keeping, they will thankfully join in the important job of keeping dry. If they feel that we really care what happens to them, it is surprising how that alone will help. The next important thing is the follow-up.

Most people need encouragement to continue with the protracted exercises and retraining programmes. Incontinence that has gone on for years is not going to be cured in weeks and it could be some months before any improvement is seen. It is in this period that encouragement is so necessary. Health education leaflets are available from the Disabled Living Foundation and are probably also available from the District Health Education Officer.

Useful Incontinence Aids

Aids are designed to do three things — to keep people dry, to help them maintain their dignity and self-respect and to help them and their family cope with the situation. The first priority with incontinence is to get a medical opinion as to its cause. The second is to get a good toilet habit established, and for this a pocket timer will be a considerable help. Only then should other items receive priority.

PROTECTING THE BED

To keep the bed dry a waterproof mattress cover or large plastic sheet will at least protect the mattress. To protect the patient, disposable underpads, of which the Polyweb is a particularly good example, are almost standard equipment. The disadvantages are that confused people tend to tear them or throw them out of the bed and restless people get them creased and torn. They need to be in direct contact with the patient to be effective. There is no use dressing an elderly person and then sitting them on an incontinent underpad on a chair.

A Kylie sheet is a washable sheet made from absorbent material which allows urine to spread across its length and prevents the urine from gathering in a pool underneath the patient. It keeps the patient dry and can be tucked under the mattress at both sides like a draw sheet. In fact it combines the principle of draw sheet and underpad. These sheets are comfortable and very absorbent.

PROTECTIVE CLOTHING

There are many very good pants on the market. One of the best known products and of proven ability are Kanga pants. The urine goes through the garment and is absorbed by the pad which is in a plastic pocket on the outside. They need to be well fitting and can then be worn with complete confidence. The Kanga male pants have a fly opening and the styling of male undergarments. They enable the wearer to use the toilet as normal, yet give protection if needed.

Other makes of pants such as the Maxi-stretch have larger pads and some people use this sort at night for extra protection.

COMMODES

For the person who cannot move very quickly, or who has an urgency to pass urine, or simply for those elderly who are not safe moving around in the night, a night commode by the bedside could save a lot of distress and possibly the occasional fractured femur. Commodes need not look like moveable lavatories. They can be functional and acceptable in appearance.

URINALS

The male 'bottle' is as well known as the bedpan, but there are now some excellent female urinals about which are not so widely known. The Suba-Seal is a light, plastic, non-spill shallow dish. It empties by removing the cap from the top of the handle. It can hold a pint of fluid and is fairly easy for the patient to manipulate herself. The Feminal is a small urinal which is used attached to a plastic bag. It can be used in the sitting or standing positions. If it is not possible for the plastic bag to be emptied immediately, the bag can be secured with a twist tie. The St Peter's Boat is a plastic boat-shaped dish for use in the standing position. Women who need to urinate frequently and cannot get to the toilet in time could find these very useful.

URINARY APPLIANCES

Indwelling catheters are small soft plastic tubes inserted into the bladder and held there by an internal cuff which is inflated from outside using an ordinary syringe; this cuff prevents the tube from falling out. The tube is then connected to a disposable bag which collects the urine.

These catheters are used by people who have lost nervous control of the bladder, for example paraplegics. They also provide an alternative for the elderly patient with intractable incontinence. The decision to use an indwelling catheter should be taken by the doctor and the patient or the family. One must weigh up the possibility of urinary infection against the damage to the skin of constant contact with urine. Sometimes the use of an indwelling catheter is the only way in which a family can cope.

There are many types of urinary appliance on the market for men. One or two firms are experimenting with female urinary appliances, but, with the anatomical differences in mind, it is easier to fit a device to males. Most of them need to be fitted by an expert fitter and for some people they work very well. A very simple, but very satisfactory one is the Posey Incontinence Sheath, which is held in place by a special sheath holder; this is available on prescription from a GP.

Some districts will offer an incontinence laundry service. Usually the clothing and bedding is collected, washed, dried and returned. Removing the wet and soiled linen from the house not only relieves the patient and family of endless washing but it also lessens the smell and makes life a bit more bearable and dignified.

Most of the aids for incontinence mentioned in the preceding sections are available free from the GP, the health authority or the social services department. The district nurse or health visitor will be able to advise on most of the aids and how and where to get them.

FAECAL INCONTINENCE

While on the subject of incontinence, there can be few greater social disabilities than that of faecal incontinence. Impaction with overflow is easily treated, but the retraining of the bowel may be long and protracted. However long it takes, though, it is well worth the effort. Faecal incontinence due to sphincter damage is not so easily cured but should always be referred to a surgeon in the hope that it can be helped by surgical intravention. If it is due to confusion or cerebrovascular disease then the caring relatives can be advised on toileting.

For relatives caring for elderly people suffering with this disorder, life can quickly become sordid and wretched while they cope with unending foul washing and fetid smells. For the sufferer it can be a degrading and ignominious existence and one which makes them withdraw from social contact. They may as well have a bell hanging from their person and go round shouting, 'Unclean, Unclean'. Research on dementia has shown that while urinary incontinence was well tolerated by families, faecal incontinence was markedly less tolerated.

Alcoholism

AVAILABILITY OF ALCOHOL

It is only in comparatively recent years that alcohol has been so freely available. Thirty years ago alcohol was sold only in public houses and in off-licence shops. Now every grocery store in the high street has shelves full of the stuff. It is not only acceptable but expected that we drink wine with our meals, have aperitifs before and liqueurs after, and it is by no means unusual for us to have stocks of wine, beers and spirits in the house. A look at the young people rampaging through the streets after football matches every Saturday will bring its own conclusion as to the effects of this easy access to excess.

However, it is not only the young who have been affected by this easy availability of alcohol. The elderly lady, who previously would not have dreamed of going into a pub or off-licence, can now pick up her bottle or two of sherry or whisky with her shopping. If she shops several times a week, she can stock up each time.

ALCOHOL DEPENDENCE IN THE ELDERLY

Keith Rix (1979) talks about the difference between an alcohol-dependent person, that is someone who has a physical dependence on alcohol and a compelling need to drink, and a second type, who he says has alcohol-related disabilities, that is people who suffer from some physical, psychological or social troubles in relation to their use of alcohol without necessarily being alcohol dependent.

Alcoholism certainly touches all age groups and all social classes, but in the elderly the resultant confusion, the risk of falls, and the danger of over-medication due to incompatibility place them at extra risk. Tolerance of alcohol decreases with age and the elderly need clear heads and steady limbs if they are to avoid the dreaded falls and confusion.

THE ALCOHOL-DEPENDENT PERSON

"One of my early introductions to the problems of alcoholism was when I was requested by a GP to do a burns dressing on a lady who had scalded her arm. She was, he said, a little bizarre, but harmless and she tended to drink a little more than she should. The door, he continued, would be open, 'Just shout and walk in.'

The address was in one of the more expensive blocks of flats and it all looked rather grand. I opened the door, shouted and walked in and it didn't look very grand any more. The patient was lying on the settee, a sherry bottle on the floor beside her and a half full tumbler of sherry on a table within easy reach. The whole place was tatty. Bottles, mostly sherry bottles, were to be found in every room; there was even one conveniently placed on the floor of the loo.

She was about 70, dishevelled and bleary-eyed, dressed after a fashion in an underslip and a voluminous silk dressing gown, which was miles too big for her. She was also very well endowed and every time she moved, great lumps of her escaped from the dressing gown. She talked non-stop in a derisory way about everyone and everything, including the government's inability to control the working classes and the GP's lack of skill and manners — the latter because he did not shake hands with her.

'You can always tell a gentleman, my dear, by his handshake.'

Her most frequently recurring theme was the avariciousness of the local off-licence.

'A disgusting mania for money'; from which I gathered that she had not paid her last bill and they had cut off her supply.

Sentences ran into each other.

'My brother died in the DTs you know but it wasn't his fault, my father was a dipsomaniac, are you passing the off-licence by any chance when you leave here?'

Her next of kin, a son, lived quite near. I telephoned him later in the day to say I thought his mother could do with a little help. The resigned tone in his voice said it all.

'Thank you,' he said, 'for telling me.' I knew he was not in the least thankful and I remembered feeling very grateful that she was not my mother."

Since then I have met many alcoholics and I have never ceased to be sorry for their families. But being sorry is not enough.

THE PERSON WITH ALCOHOL-RELATED DISABILITIES

Most alcoholic problems in the elderly arise because they fall into Dr Rix's second category; they have alcohol-related disabilities. They are not physically dependent on alcohol; they use it as a crutch to overcome their depression, loneliness, isolation and despair, and that is something that we can and should do something about. If they can be involved with neighbours, clubs and friendly visitors, and their supply curtailed, then there is a good chance that they will have long periods when they can control their drinking.

It would be foolish to think that they will all become as sober as the proverbial judge, but even 2-3 months on the wagon is worth working for and their relatives are always grateful for a respite.

"One such case was Mrs Grant. She lived in a very pleasant little town house in the centre of the town, an area well served with public houses. Fortunately, her husband, before he died, had tied up her money in a trust fund so that she could only spend the interest and not the capital. The interest was more than adequate for normal needs but she was a very sociable old girl and whenever she went for a drink she tended to invite the entire custom of the local pub to join her.

In her cups she also invited all the local drop-outs to drop in, so that you never quite knew who you were likely to meet in the house. Her unfortunate son and grandsons spent a lot of time retrieving her from one crisis after another. Over the years she became less mobile and less exuberant. When sober she was always charming; when in her cups she would cry, hiccough and slobber. She would take to her bed and become incontinent. The trigger factor could range from one of her friends leaving, to one of her drunken squatters breaking the door down because he had forgotten his key, to a letter from her son saying he was not prepared to pay a particular bill.

There was a repeating pattern to it all. The crisis would arise. If it was not solved fairly quickly then Mrs Grant would retire into alcoholic oblivion. Then would come the maudlin stage, the drying out in the nursing home and the promise that it would never happen again. Then she would return home, with all the services laid on, to a house that was once again squatter free. Sometimes this was followed up by months of sobriety until the next upset and the whole unhappy circle would start again."

She used alcohol as a crutch, just like some people use antidepressants and tranquillisers. She was not physically dependent on it, because once happy again she could and did go many months without getting drunk. Mrs Grant was a slightly larger than life example of the person who drinks to cover up their other problems. There are many elderly people who drink secretly and steadily through bottle after bottle of liquor to hide — both to themselves and to the world at large — that they are lonely and frightened. They would gladly replace alcohol by friends, visitors and company.

Loneliness and Isolation

Loneliness, as we all know, is quite a different thing to being alone. To be alone, to be solitary, can be for some people a blissful state. As Justice Louis D. Brandeis said, 'The right to be left alone is the most comprehensive of rights and the right most valued in civilised man' (see *Bartlett's Quotations*). A great many people not only enjoy being alone but fight vigorously to maintain that right.

Loneliness, on the other hand, is the feeling of unhappiness because one is left without the companionship of others; and isolation, in a social sense, is a lack of contact between persons, or groups — the failure of genuine communication and interaction with others.

Loneliness and isolation can be as hard for the young adult in the big city as they can for the elderly person. The difference is that the young adult will find interaction in his working life, a factor which the elderly person no longer has available to him or her. A great deal of loneliness in the old is caused by the death of the partner. It is the norm for women to marry men older than themselves. It is also the norm that women have, on average, a longer life span, so it is not surprising that most women outlive their husbands. It is harder for the aged to make new friends, or indeed to get over the death of someone they have lived with for 40 or 50 years. Depression, sometimes the natural result of bereavement, or of any loss, may be the cause of further loneliness as people shy away from the misery and distress associated with it.

THE ELDERLY WHO LIVE ALONE

In 1971 I carried out a small study of the elderly living alone which focused particularly on nutrition (Brown, 1971). The elderly, particularly those living alone, are often said to be 'at risk' of malnutrition. It is difficult to think of malnutrition in our affluent society. We are constantly being reminded that we overeat and under-exercise. We eat more sugar per head of population than most countries and we eat more sweets per head of population than any country in the world. It was difficult to imagine that among all the affluent, fat, sweet-toothed population there was a minority group who did not have enough to eat.

My survey was carried out among a community of old people living in sheltered accommodation. The reason for choosing that particular group was that they were all elderly, they all lived alone, and they were all in the lower socio-economic class. Exton-Smith (1965) gives the main causes of malnutrition in the elderly as follows: ignorance (such as when a man is left to cater for himself), loneliness and social isolation, mental disturbance, physical disability, loss of appetite, poverty, ill-fitting dentures and alcoholism.

I did not find a great deal of malnutrition during my survey, although some of the old people ate a boring and monotonous diet. What did surprise me was the amount of loneliness I found. I had included a question on the amount of contact they had with their neighbours because Exton-Smith had given loneliness and social isolation as one of the main causes of malnutrition. I did not expect to find a great deal of it in an area of sheltered accommodation which housed 120 people in close proximity to each other. Only 35 per cent were living happy fulfilled lives. Another 30 per cent had a reasonable amount of contact, but it was mostly with outside friends and relatives. Within the community, some of this group lived in 'splendid isolation'.

A large proportion of those surveyed, some 35 per cent, felt some isolation and loneliness. These were the ones who sat waiting for someone else to make the first move. These were the ones who fondly showed me photographs of friends and relatives, now dead or too far away to visit. A large number of them were single and with no immediate family. Some of them had disabilities which confined them to home; some just sitting, waiting. For them malnutrition, illness and poverty all paled into insignificance beside the question of sheer loneliness, of having nothing to do and no one to do it with. It must be very demoralising to wake up in the morning and realise that nobody cares if you get up, whether you eat or not, in fact whether you live or not. One old lady said to me, 'The thing that I find most distressing is the knowledge that when I die there will nobody at my funeral; there is no one left to care.'

The development of consultative health clinics and special screening clinics for the elderly and the establishment of geriatric health visitors will all help in the early diagnosis of disability, including malnutrition. Early diagnosis and treatment will not be of much use, however, if the elderly person has then got to return to an isolated position within the community. We must involve the community in the care of its elderly. We must involve voluntary organisations, senior school children and church groups — if we can, get them to visit the old; if we can, encourage the elderly to visit each other; if we can, just show them that we care enough to do something.

As a result of my survey, a small group of people got together and formed a club, using as a meeting place a lounge that had fortunately been incorporated in one of the blocks of flatlets. Up to that time the lounge had remained in a virginal and untouched state. The elderly tenants came in slowly and gradually. They were asked to name their club and they chose 'The Welcome Club'.

Now they run many of the functions themselves; bingo, whist and craft afternoons are favourite sessions. They run a little shop, which one of the committee keeps stocked up for them. One of the members, an 83 year old, keeps a birthday book and on every member's birthday she delivers a greetings card so that they know that someone has remembered. Many of them have taken to giving little tea parties in the club lounge on their birthdays and there is always a bit of healthy competition to see who bakes a better cake.

A monthly newsletter keeps them all in touch with forthcoming entertainments. There are many concert groups who delight in giving shows for the members and they are always well attended. In the summer months, coach and theatre outings cause great excitement and sometimes great arguments, but even argumentive interaction is good in that they are at least communicating with each other. The surprising and very pleasant outcome has been the amount of work and the high degree of involvement which the members themselves put into the club. There is a feeling of usefulness and a purpose once again which involves things like self-respect, self-esteem and confidence in their own ability. Albert Schweitzer once said, 'There is no higher religion than human service. To work for the common good is the greatest creed' (see Peter, 1977).

Hypothermia – Cold Kills the Old

Hypothermia, that modish and mysterious condition, so serious to the elderly and the very young infant, in which the body is unable to maintain the necessary temperature, is becoming well known to everyone dealing with the elderly. It is not only in old houses, where the heating systems and appliances are past their best, where the wind whistles through unclosable windows, under gaps in the doors and up open chimneys, taking any warm air it can find with it, that we need to be concerned. Elderly people, if left sitting for long periods even in warm hospital wards, can become cold. We are surprised that they feel cold in their nightdress and dressing gown because we tend to forget that older people are used to wearing layers of woollen undergarments.

WHAT IS HYPOTHERMIA?

Hypothermia is a low body temperature, that is one below 35 °C (95 °F), but the body has different temperatures in different places. Wicks (1978) talks about the varying degrees of temperature on the body surface and that of the inner body or 'core', and he reminds us that: 'The most important temperatures to maintain at an adequate level are those of the deep body or core.'

Hypothermia then is an abnormality in body temperature in which a fall below 35 °C would be considered serious. Temperatures have been recorded as low as 21 °C (Agate, 1970). It will come as no surprise to most people that those most at risk are the older pensioners, who are in receipt of supplementary benefit, are underweight and are living in older houses. However, hypothermia, like many other social diseases does not confine itself to social class 4 or 5.

"Miss Evans was an 86 year old living in a large, three-bedroomed semi-detached house. Her housekeeper and dear friend, a 56 year old, strong, healthy woman, died suddenly from a stroke, leaving poor Miss Evans without a relative or near friend. Miss Evans was poor in the sense of having no relatives, not in the financial sense. She was very well endowed with this world's goods.

After the death of her housekeeper, Miss Evans was very bereft and wandered vaguely around for months. Her house got colder and colder. She refused to have more than one bar of her electric fire on. She always maintained that if she had any more heat on she felt too hot and uncomfortable — and indeed her hands always felt warm. She refused to have her bed brought downstairs because she had always gone upstairs to bed and she would not have any heating in her bedroom because she had never done so in the past. When it was pointed out to her that she had never been 86 years old before, she said it was irrelevant.

She became slightly confused, a little pale, and was sitting in a drowsy way. It was at this stage that someone had the bright idea of taking her temperature with a low-reading thermometer. Despite her warm hands, the thermometer read 33°C."

LOW-READING THERMOMETERS

Dr Geoffrey Taylor, whose interest in hypothermia has done so much to make the caring professions and the public aware of its problems and dangers, speaking of the usual type of thermometer, has said, 'It seems that we have all failed to recognise hypothermia, because the clinical thermometer, for historical and arbitrary reasons, does not record it' (Taylor, 1964).

The standard thermometer begins to register at 35 °C (95 °F) and is for obvious reasons useless in diagnosing hypothermia. The low-reading thermometer, which begins to register at 23.9 °C (75 °F) and reads up to 40.6 °C (105 °F), is now much more commonly used among community nurses and should be utilised by everyone who deals with the elderly.

Still battling on with his crusade, Taylor (1981) also suggests that a district nurse's equipment for prevention of hypothermia is a low-reading thermometer, a household thermometer and a draught excluder. He could have well added an electric blanket and a good warm pair of bed-socks. For any elderly person, a sausage-shaped draught excluder and a pair of bed-socks would make an ideal present.

WHY WON'T OLD PEOPLE HEAT THEIR HOMES?

Why, oh why won't elderly people heat their homes adequately? Well, to begin with, they may not be able to afford the high cost of heating. If they use coal fires there is the job of going out into the cold to fill the coal bucket. If it is cold and dark outside, they are even less likely to venture out. Many old houses, believe it or not, still have outside toilets, and going out to them can be a chilling business. Even if they have the money, many of them have an ingrained horror of waste and heating comes under the heading of waste for many. They are less likely to be aware

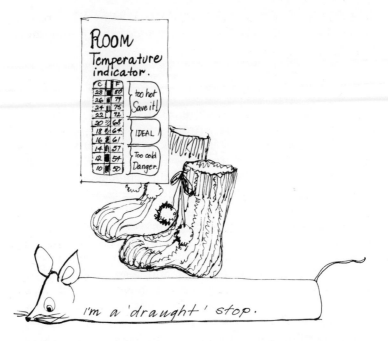

of cold because they have never been used to things like central heating. Their expectations of comfort are not as high as those of younger people, who have been brought up to believe that certain standards are theirs by right; indeed elderly people's tolerance of cold does seem to be higher than most of ours.

DIAGNOSING HYPOTHERMIA

Most literature on the subject says that the way to diagnose hypothermia is to take the rectal temperature for 5 minutes with a low-reading thermometer, or to feel those places which are normally always warm, like the abdominal wall or the inside of the thighs. In the hypothermic person these places will be cold.

This is very sound advice except that as a preventative measure it might be a little difficult. Most elderly people would take exception to any of these manoeuvres and it might, initially at least, be more prudent to stick to the orthodox approach of taking the oral temperature.

The Elderly and Problems of Physical Abuse

MUGGING

Although mugging may be thought of, and spoken of, as a new type of crime, there is, in fact, little new about it other than its name. The term 'mugging' comes from America, where 'to mug' means to attack an easy victim. It is a crime that has attracted a great deal of publicity in the 1970s and 1980s and has entered our language as a verb (to mug) with the meanings assault, attack, knock down, strong-arm, throttle, garrotte, choke, rob, steal from.

All these violent actions were attributed, in previous times, to footpads, highwaymen, bandits, the Parisian *apache,* the famous, or to be more precise the infamous, garrotters of the 19th century, and in more recent times to outlaws, gangsters, thugs and hoodlums.

Crimes of robbery with violence or assaults with intent to rob are not new, but if the newspapers and television reports are anything to go by they are on the increase. The new-style mugging would appear to be a crime of youth, sometimes of extreme youth. Whatever the sociological and psychological reasons for its increase and the younger age of its perpetrators, there is no doubt that the easiest 'mug' of all is the frail, elderly person, walking alone. It is probably this aspect of mugging that has brought about such a revulsion for the crime in the minds of most people.

EFFECTS OF CRIME ON THE ELDERLY

Even a minor criminal incident against an old person can be shattering and can cause distress and after-effects out of all proportion to the crime. Todd (1981) points out that 'Even a minor burglary can cause enormous distress because the victim's personal territory has been violated'.

The snatched handbag can lead to a fall which may cause a fracture, and this may mean a complete change in life-style. A burglary, however minor, can lead to a sense of fear and insecurity in case 'they' come back. Articles stolen may be treasured for their memories rather than their financial value. Distress and anxiety after the offence can lead elderly people to lock themselves up in their rooms, thereby restricting their activities and social outlets.

WHAT IS THE INCIDENCE OF CRIME AGAINST THE ELDERLY?

There are no national statistics because the ages of victims are not recorded. However, recent surveys suggest that less than 10 per cent of the elderly population are troubled by criminal activities, and of those who had been affected, most reported incidences were of a very minor nature such as theft of milk bottles.

American surveys indicate a great fear among their elderly who live in big cities. In fact the fear of mugging has overtaken ill-health as one of the fears of old-age. Gornick (1978) says, 'The Eskimos put their people out on ice floes when they get too old to work and the nomads simply leave them behind when they move on, but we hunt them in packs.'

The effects of all the publicity, both from America and in our own media — where attacks on old people and young children always make good copy — could well cause a dichotomy for old people. While it may make them more aware and more alert to the dangers, it can also give them the impression that crime is increasing at an alarming rate and that they are not safe anywhere. It is necessary to keep a sense of proportion about the risk involved, and while it is good to take sensible precautions it would be foolish to allow a fear of mugging to alter their way of life.

PRECAUTIONS

The elderly should be warned against carrying items of value or important papers with them. One elderly lady carried her will around in her bag so that if she died suddenly someone would know what she wished done with her estate. The will gave detailed information on where in her home she had hidden items of great value and where, in the garden, she had buried the box with the money.

Old people should be encouraged not to have more money on their person than they need for their immediate use and they should try to alter their habits and routines occasionally. If they leave their homes every Tuesday morning at 10 a.m. to collect their pension and return at exactly 12 noon, they are more likely to attract unwelcome attention. Above all they have nothing to gain by trying to resist the young thugs who attack them except injury. Better to lose a small amount of money than your life or the ability to walk again.

The elderly are very liable to be exploited by doorstep 'con' men who offer to do odd jobs or buy furniture. Some gain easy access by saying they are from the gas or electricity company. The act of carrying a clip-board would seem to offer an 'open sesame' into most people's homes. In 15 years of knocking on doors I have never once been asked to prove my identity. A door-chain and the request for official identification will get rid of bogus gas-men quicker than anything.

The police force is always happy to advise on security and they will give talks to clubs and societies on crime prevention. If elderly people go out in the evening they should leave a light on as it acts as a deterrent, but probably the best deterrent of all to both the mugger and the thief is the loud barking of a dog. For a lot of elderly people living alone their dog is not only their friend and pet but also their protector.

Victim support schemes are run by volunteers in many parts of the country. They provide counselling and practical help for those who have been the victims of crime, including the elderly. They will help with clearing up the mess, with insurance claim forms and with applications to the Criminal Injuries Compensation Board.

GRANNY BASHING

Abuse of the elderly does not have any hard statistics to support it, unlike non-accidental injury to children, which has been extensively documented. To begin with, elderly people do not generate the sort of stress that a screaming baby does. The stress the elderly beget is more likely to be a gradual build-up of frustration and irritation. Neither is it as easy to knock an adult about as it is a child, and those who burn and maim children probably would not feel the same about crippling an adult, however old and defenceless.

It is doubtful, therefore, if many people are consciously determined to beat up their elderly, but what can happen is that the carer runs out of patience and tolerance and that the elderly person may be subjected to verbal rather than physical violence.

We all have a threshold for stress as well as pain. Some, stoically, can tolerate a high degree of irritation and annoyance. For others, the blast-off point comes quickly. There is no use or point in the professional being annoyed at the inability of relatives to cope. If their stress level is a low one, they will either shout for help or crack and go under. It takes a very special kind of tolerance to cope with a shambling, demented relative, who follows you about the house all day asking the same question over and over again; or the exasperation of finding wet patches on your best chairs; or the frustration of broken sleep because the elderly relative feels the need to be helped out of bed to the toilet every few hours during the night.

It is remarkable too that we always seem to tolerate other people's relatives better than our own. Could it be that we don't have guilt feelings about other peoples' relatives, or could it be that we actually feel a bit 'holier than thou' because we are doing the caring? Whatever the reason, it is unfortunate that it does tend to make us a mite less than tolerant of those relatives who cannot cope.

Mr and Mrs Lesson and their 18 month old daughter, Caroline, lived in a little terraced three-bedroomed house. It has a pocket-sized back garden and no front garden, the front door opening on to the road. Living with them was Mrs Lesson's 69 year old mother, Mrs Fry, who unfortunately suffered from senile dementia. Once a year, as a great favour, one of Mrs Lesson's brothers would take their mother for 2 weeks to give the Lessons a break.

As Caroline got bigger and more adventurous Mrs Lesson found it more difficult to cope. Poor Mrs Fry, in an endeavour to be helpful, would do things for Caroline which were not in her best interests, like opening the front door to let her out. Mrs Lesson found she was always in demand; if it was not Caroline, it was her mother. Both of them followed her around talking their own kind of gibberish. She found herself frequently shouting at them, which made them cry and her feel guilty.

Mrs Fry was not incontinent but felt she always wanted to go to the toilet, and talked endlessly about it. Caroline picked the line up from Gran and also insisted that she too wanted to use her potty all the time. The stress factors slowly built up. Mr Lesson took to doing more overtime, which kept him safely away from the house but left Mrs Lesson on her own in the evenings when she might have got a bit of relief. The final straw came when she realised she was pregnant, despite her IUD.

Something had to go, and in this case it was Mrs Fry. She went into day care 2 days a week, gradually increasing as Mrs Lesson's pregnancy advanced. Before the second baby was born Mrs Fry was in full time care, but going home to the Lesson family every Sunday for the day.

RELIEF FOR THE FAMILY

The social services department provides day care facilities in most of their homes. Unfortunately the supply never quite meets the demand, but they cope with a large number of referrals. Some people prefer to use the private sector and there are nursing and rest homes which will take elderly day care cases. The voluntary organisations also have many clubs; some have transport facilities and will pick up people and transport them home.

Day hospitals also care for people on a regular 'nine to five' basis, but not many of them will accept people just because of social need. They tend to see their objectives as retraining and curative. Admission to day hospitals are usually the result of a GP referring an old person to a hospital's geriatric department.

Short stay care of 2-3 weeks to give the family a rest or to allow them to take a holiday is available through social services departments and hospitals, but needs to be requested well in advance. Some hospitals have schemes which allow elderly people who need long term nursing care to spend alternate months in hospital and at home.

The relatives who find that their stress threshold is getting lower and their ability to handle the situation is slipping away from them should always shout for help. There is a very thin line between normal and firm handling, and an even thinner one between firm and rough handling.

Physical abuse of the elderly is, quite rightly, viewed with horror and repugnance by the general public. We can't prevent old age. We can't prevent many of the conditions that makes life sad and painful for some old people, but we can prevent them being abused, victimised, conned, intimidated, mugged and degraded. We owe them that at least.

Conclusions

This chapter has examined a number of practical ways of overcoming the difficulties and problems which the elderly may encounter.

Incontinence, the greatest social stigma of all time, is said to inflict some 17 million people in the UK alone. What a chance for the caring professions to help so many! While we are quite good at explaining to relatives practical things like the best position to place a commode in a bedroom or how to care for a Kylie sheet, we are sometimes woefully inadequate in giving moral support to both clients and relatives.

Alcoholism, which destroys inhibitions and can make our behaviour ridiculous, is even more destructive to the aged. Emotional tearful alcoholics are a bore at any age, but in the elderly it can be so pathetic that people tend to give them a wide berth. Their subsequent isolation is all the more demoralising and their falls, unlike those of the young, can be the beginning of a sad end. For the large number who are not alcohol dependent there is a strong chance that social intervention may change their life-style, and we owe them at least that chance.

Most of us have at sometime or other felt lonely, if only for a short period, but try to imagine that loneliness becoming desolate nothingness, stretching on into weeks and months and years: 'To be old and helpless is unfortunate, to be old, helpless and alone is heartbreaking.' It deserves more from us than giving an isolated old person a list of clubs they can visit. If they were capable of that they would not be sitting at home in the first place. For the isolated person, the first visit to a club takes courage; a courage few will be able to muster unless they have the strong physical support of someone who will actually take them and introduce them into the new surroundings. Indeed it may take six or seven such introductions before they feel secure enough to go alone. It is not easy for the supporter; at times it can even be frustrating, vexatious or downright maddening, but it's always worth trying.

A gentle reminder is needed that the winter is not time to start an economy drive for the older members of the family, and it is much better to be warm than dead. The old maxim that there are no pockets in a shroud is never more true than in cases where the home is as cold as the grave. The important thing to remember about hypothermia is that cold really does kill the old.

Abuse of the elderly, be it physical, verbal or mental, is as much an attack upon their dignity as upon their person. When we lose our dignity we lose our feeling of belonging, of being part of our fellow men. We all need to belong and to feel respected. As we get older, we too will need constructive help to overcome many of the problems outlined in this chapter.

References

Agate, J. (1978). *Geriatrics for Nurses and Social Workers,* Heinemann, London.

Bartlett's Quotations, Macmillan, London.

Brown, P. (1971). A study of the aged living alone, with special emphasis on nutrition (unpublished).

Exton-Smith, A. N. (1965). Report of an investigation into the dietary requirements of elderly women living alone.

Report prepared for the King Edward Fund for London.
Gornick, N. (1978). For the rest of our days, things can only get worse. In *The New Old — A Struggle for Decent Aging* (Eds R. Gross, B. Gross and S. Seidman), Anchor Books, New York, pp. 28-37.
Hood, N. A. (1980). Some guidance beyond the incontinence pad. *Geriatric Medicine*, 10 (6), 59-62.
Peter, L. (1977). *Quotations for Our Time*, Methuen Paperbacks, London.
Rix, B. (1979). How to recognize and help the elderly alcoholic. *Geriatric Medicine*, 9 (11), 75-77.
Taylor, G. (1964). The problems of hypothermia in the elderly. *The Practitioner*, 193, 761-767.
Taylor, G. (1981). Meet Dr Hypothermia. *Nursing Times*, 77 (3), 100.
Todd, H. (1981). Elderly victims of crime. *Geriatric Medicine*, 11 (1), 80-83.
Wicks, M. (1978). *Old and Cold*, Heinemann, London.

Useful Addresses

Incontinence Advisory Service, Disabled Living Foundation, 346 High Street, Kensington, London.
Kanga Hospital Products Ltd, PO Box 39, Bentinck Street, Bolton (*Kanga pants*).
Martin Creasey Ltd, 89 Clumber Street, Hull (*Posey male incontinence sheath and holder*).
Nicholas Laboratories Ltd, 225 Bath Road, Slough (*Kylie sheets*).
Smith and Nephew Medical Ltd, Woodlands Road, Birmingham (*Polyweb*).
William Freeman and Co. Ltd, Suba-Seal Works, Staincross, Barnsley, Yorkshire (*Suba-Seal, Feminal, St Peter's Boat*).

6 Mental Illness in the Elderly

Introduction

The world of the mentally ill is one into which few of us venture. Most people know little of psychiatry other than the well known jokes: 'A psychiatrist is a man who goes to the Folies Bergère and looks at the audience.' 'A neurotic is a man who builds castles in the air, psychotics live in them and psychiatrists collect the rent.' This ignorance can make people fearful of the mentally ill and even the people who care for them. It is easy to develop irrational fears that the mentally ill will attack us or others, and that it will not be possible to control the situation. There are also fears associated with their less bizarre behaviour. For example, the mentally ill are untidy in that they do not stay in one place like the physically ill — they wander, they roam, they forget how important we and our treatments are. Above all, they are difficult to 'cure' and we do so like to tidy things up and see a finished product.

Unlike the eccentric and the recluse, who although considered oddities are mentally aware of who they are, what they are doing and why they are doing it, the mentally frail or ill do not have that sort of hold on life. They can be bemused, confused, depressed, bewildered, uncertain, or just plain muddled. They are pitiable, yet irritating. If we are not afraid of them we tend to treat them like children, even to the extent of deciding where and how they will live. We put them in 'homes' and hospitals, with or without their consent, and tell ourselves that we are doing it in their best interests. The fact that it might just be in our best interests to get them off our patch is something we do not easily admit to. Fortunately the laws on mental health do not allow for indiscriminate 'putting away'. This chapter explores all the problems outlined above, frequently drawing upon my own experience working with the elderly in the community, and there is also some practical assistance on understanding the appropriate parts of the Mental Health Act.

Statistics are Thin on the Ground

While there is no difficulty in getting opinions and assumptions about the number of elderly people in the community suffering from mental illness, it is very difficult to get hold of hard facts. It is easy to see why the difficulty exists because it is one thing to hold Gallup polls on politics, cat food or TV programmes, but it is quite another thing to ask people if they or their spouse happen to be mentally ill. Moreover, it is very difficult to define mental illness — where does eccentricity end and mental illness begin, for example?

In the often quoted survey of Kay, Beamish and Roth (1964) it is suggested that 41 per cent of elderly people living at home have some psychiatric abnormality. One can't help feeling that if they carried out a similar survey in any age group of people that they would find the same level of psychiatric abnormalities — depending, that is, on what 'abnormal' means! It is easy to see oddness in other people that we can't see in ourselves. We use expressions about people to indicate what we think of their mental ability: 'There's more out than in', 'There's nowt as queer as folk', 'He's as nutty as a fruit cake', 'I get anxious — you get paranoiac', 'I'm tidy — you are obsessional'.

Of course there is bound to be a high proportion of illness among the elderly, both physical and mental, and of course many old people in the community are ill. However, if we look at some of the symptoms used by Kay, Beamish and Roth to indicate psychiatric abnormality, then the figure is understandable: spells of depression, anxiety, tension or irritability, panic attacks, hysteria and hypochondriacal preoccupations. How many times have we all run the gauntlet of that little lot without thinking of ourselves as being particularly psychotic.

It is estimated that half the beds in both mental and general hospitals are filled with the over-65s, and it is probably true, but it is something we should all be ashamed of because many of them need not be there at all. Let us not blame the elderly for occupying the beds, rather let us look for better caring facilities outside the hospital environment and better facilities to keep them in their homes — where they would prefer to be.

Understanding the Mentally Frail

Mental illness in the elderly has now become a speciality in its own right under the term 'psychogeriatrics.' The title 'psychogeriatrician' puts one in mind of psychotic geriatric consultants running round, hearing voices and seeing visions! However, it is important that health districts should have an appointed specialist in this field, with, and this is the most important thing of all, beds in hospital to call his own.

I feel sure that the majority of people who work in the community are, like myself, extremely hazy when it comes to the mentally ill patient. We simply do not know how to cope with the psychotic, neurotic, depressive, dementive and confused, nor do we know how to differentiate between them. We would find it difficult to know whether someone was suffering from delirium, dementia or depression or a mixture of all three. All we can hope to do is to recognise the abnormal and to refer the patient on, through their GP, to the appropriate department.

On the other hand, most of us who spend our working life going in and out of other people's homes do, over the years, develop our own kind of 'diagnostic slide rule'. When elderly people start acting out of character I find it very worthwhile to sit down and listen. A half-hour spent listening and gently probing can save many hours of work later.

My 'slide rule' runs to very simple things:

(1) Have they changed their habits, and if so, why?

(2) Have they changed their drugs? A new young, terribly keen GP might prescribe an enlarged battery of drugs, and that could lead to a complete change in behaviour.

(3) Has the 'little drop' taken for medicinal purposes only increased for any reason? I once started a hue and cry when I found a 78 year old man crashing round his kitchen, banging a saucepan against the skirting board. The consultant

psychiatrist was very kind about it really, but he did suggest that I note the large number of empty wine bottles in future. The old gentleman was, on that occasion, as high as a kite and 'chasing mice'. Treating his alcoholism was a

long way from emergency treatment for what I took to be
his mania.

(4) Depressed people are almost never disorientated, or so
some psychiatrists believe.

(5) A rapid onset of confusion or disorientation suggests
an infection of some sort, such as penumonia or an injury
(for example, of the head).

(6) If an old person says they are being 'got at' it might
just be true.

There are of course many occasions when this 'slide rule'
does not work and when, having run through your repertoire
of clues, you are still completely at a loss. When that happens
'send for a second opinion'.

Sometimes pre-knowledge of the patients helps, but not
always. Knowing that a person has a history of mental
illness may make it difficult not to prejudge the situation
before you even visit, as the following example illustrates.

"Mrs Mac was a widow, in her late 70s, living alone, suffering from dementia. She was a great trial to her neighbours,
often wandering into their homes. Because she had lived in
the same house for many years, and because she had been a
very good neighbour in the past, most of them tolerated her.
They nearly all fed her and then returned her to her home.
Every now and then somebody would start the 'She ought
to be in a home' bit, but somehow she managed to hang on.
The next-door neighbour was particularly kind, but there
eventually came a day when even she started muttering
'Something must be done', and to reinforce her argument
she went off for a week to her married daughter's home.
Within a few days there was a spate of calls into the surgery.
Mrs Mac was wandering all over the place looking for her
friendly neighbour. Mrs Mac was accusing people of taking
her things. Mrs Mac had lost her handbag and pension book.

'They've taken all my things,' she told me, as soon as she
opened the door.

'Yes, yes,' I replied, in my patronising, we must humour
the natives, voice, leading her into the kitchen.

'All gone,' she repeated, tears flowing down her face, as
she shuffled into the front room.

102 The Other Side of Growing Older

I wandered in behind her and then stopped, open-mouthed. She was right, someone *had* taken all her things, or at least they had taken all the best bits of furniture and silver. It is despicable that people take advantage of the Mrs Macs, but it turned out that she had 'sold' her furniture for a pittance to some con men who had called at the door."

One good thing came about as a result of it, the neighbours, particularly the next-door neighbour, were so incensed at what had happened and so sorry that they had not prevented it, that they all took her under their collective wing and between them they cared for her until she died about a year later.

SOCIETY'S REACTION TO MENTAL ILLNESS

There must be many people who, probably through a lack of knowledge, suffer a degree of frustration when dealing with mental illness. We like to know the which, the why and the wherefore of things. Physical illness is easy to understand; you can do tests and you can get results. People have operations and they either get better or they don't, but there is a reason for it all. Mental illness, on the other hand, is a closed book. The phrases are familiar but they do not convey anything. Diagnosis and differentiation between the various possibilities is like talking in a foreign language. Even when the psychiatrist has put a label to the condition, it often doesn't help. We like to see the results of our caring and treating. We like to see nice, clean, well fed people tucked up in bed, getting better; or if people must die, then we like them to do it in a decent British sort of way which gives us a chance to show our skills at terminal care.

But the elderly mentally ill are not like that. They are more likely to wander round in an untidy fashion, creating problems. The depressed among them can be very depressing. They change their mind 20 times a day; they forget who you are or why they've asked you to call, and most unforgivable of all, they occasionally frighten the living daylights out of us.

FEAR OF THE MENTALLY ILL

> As I was going up the stair
> I met a man who wasn't there.
> He wasn't there again to-day,
> I wish, I wish he'd go away.

Hughes Mearns (see *Bartlett's Quotations*)

"Miss H was a single, 70 year old lady, living alone. She was referred to me, bright and early one Monday morning, by a friend of her sister. The background to the story was that Miss H had been telephoning her sister, who lived several hundred miles away. As a result of these phone calls the sister had contacted the friend and asked her to visit Miss H as she sounded most odd. The friend had dutifully visited after going to church on the Sunday, and that was why she was waiting for me to arrive in my office on Monday morning.

Miss H lived in a flat in what had been a large three-bedroomed semi-detached house, which an enterprising landlord had converted into four flatlets, each containing a large bedsittingroom and a separate kitchen and bathroom. Now it was Miss H's belief that her sister was being held against her will in one of the upstairs flats by the police. She could hear her sister crying and she therefore spent quite a lot of her time banging on the door of the flat upstairs, demanding, or alternatively pleading for her sister's release. The flat receiving all this unwelcome attention belonged to a 79 year old widow, who had a heart condition. She was so terrified that she had locked up her flat and taken refuge in a neighbour's house, and who can blame her.

A quick word with the GP and it was agreed that I would visit and get the story. The records showed that she had been registered with the practice for 18 months and that she had had a similar episode 3 years before, for which she had received psychiatric help. The various diagnoses included schizophrenia, paraphrenia and manic-depressive depression. Now they might all have been vaguely similar or vastly different conditions, but to me they all sounded serious and slightly threatening. I have been particularly apprehensive about schizophrenia since I found myself locked into a house with what the Mental Health people had called a 'burnt-out' schizophrenic, who had a great deal more fire in his belly than anyone gave him credit for.

'Fear of violence in the mentally ill is not only irrational, but unrealistic', I told myself as I walked up the path to the front door, but being a dreadful coward I'm not easy to convince, so my anxiety level was fairly high by the time I got to Flat 3.

The door to Flat 3 was open, and as I rang the bell a very smartly dressed woman, who looked to be in her early 60s, came forward and said, 'Do come in, I've been expecting you.'

The flat was very clean and elegantly furnished. Not knowing who this lady was, but assuming that she was yet another friend, neighbour or relative, I produced my card, introduced myself and waited for her to do the same, without any luck.

'Please sit down. I'd like, if I may, to explain the situation.'

I sat, but kept an eye towards the bathroom and kitchen in case our depressive, hallucinating schizophrenic should suddenly take it into her head to join us.

'It's all very difficult. You see the police are holding my sister in the flat upstairs and they are doing terrible things to her. It's so unfair, she has never done anyone any harm. Do please help me.'

My first reaction was, how can anyone look so sane and make a statement like that? My second was one of surprise that this was Miss H. Whatever her mental state, she was physically a very well looking woman and could easily have passed for a 60 year old. My third reaction was one of intense pity for the agony of mind she was going through. The pain and distress in her eyes showed only too clearly that she was living in a very private sort of hell.

'It's worse at night time. I try to stay awake to listen, but sometimes I fall asleep and then, when I do awake, they have taken her out into the garden for exercise and she cries. I've called some of the other people in the house, but they won't help me.'

My pity extended to the other tenants in the house, all of them elderly, and all no doubt fed up and frightened.

Mental illness is a bit like a pebble thrown into a pool of water, the ripples are far reaching. Already we had a very stressed and distressed Miss H, the anxious tenants of the other three flats, the frustrated neighbour who had taken the top tenant in, the landlord to whom the other tenants had started to complain, Miss H's sister, the friend, and the milkman, who contacted the surgery later on in the day. In fact the only people who seemed to be sublimely unaware of the whole thing were the much maligned police.

Meanwhile Miss H had been talking non-stop. She phoned her sister in Leeds and spoke to her several times a day, but was convinced that the police had the phone plugged into the flat upstairs. When I pointed out that there was no sound from the flat above, she had a ready answer about the craft and guile of the police. Thinking that it might put her mind at rest if she could see into the flat above, I went to the neighbour's house and asked the upstairs tenant if I might show Miss H that the flat was empty. She agreed on condition that I did not tell Miss H where she was.

Miss H did not question where I had got the keys from; all she was interested in was getting in to see her sister. We entered the empty flat; we looked in the kitchen and the bathroom; we looked under the bed, in the cupboards, and in the toilet. I was just about to lead her out when she saw the skylight leading up to the attic.

'Up there,' she cried, 'look up there.' So in the end all I had done was to convince her that not only had the police got her sister but during the day they dragged her up into the attic. As I left the house to get her GP, I remembered a psychiatrist once quoting,

A web of intrigue around me spins,
I smell it in the air.

Miss H was seen by the psychiatrist the following day, diagnosed as a paraphrenic and accepted treatment of Flupenthixol injections administered by the community psychiatric nurse. Her explanation was that her sister was eventually allowed home, and she never accepted the fact that she had been hallucinating. I don't know how the psychiatrist had got her to accept treatment, but gradually she improved. However, when I visited the house later in the year, I noticed that the other three tenants had changed. About 9 months later she was admitted to the psychiatric hospital under 'a section' and died there."

How can the mind do this to people? It is strange that the brain, which in terms of body weight is a small organ, has the power to destroy someone's personality like that. Why is it that some people have to go through the agony of actually seeing and hearing things that are not there, and why is it that many of us are so irrationally afraid of them?

Perhaps the greatest fear of all is that the dreaded senile dementia might strike within our own circle, that it might happen to someone we have known, loved and respected. It is awful to see one's parents dribbling or incontinent, or behaving in an uninhibited way, or flying into a rage and accusing the family of robbing them, or to watch a beloved mother, father, aunt or grandparent disintegrate before your very eyes. It is easy to pity them, but to pity yourself more; to feel love, sympathy, guilt and resentment all at the same time, and above all, to fear that it might be hereditary and that you might end up like that yourself. These are the sort of fears that should make us professionally aware of the very poor facilities available, and make us start shouting on other people's behalf.

Dementia – Alzheimer's Disease

Dementia is an insidious and irreversible destruction of brain tissue. In *Dementia in Old Age* (1979) the Office of Health Economics differentiates between dementia and Alzheimer's disease as follows: 'Dementia is something that happens in old age, while Alzheimer's disease is a form of dementia occurring earlier in life'. However, there is obviously room for debate here, since Behan (1981) said that 'senile dementia, pre-senile dementia and Alzheimer's disease are synonymous terms'.

Dementia accounts for about 70 per cent of all cases studied at post mortem; arteriosclerotic dementia (or multi-infarct dementia) accounts for about 20 per cent and chronic alcoholism, metabolic disorders and inherited diseases account for the remainder.

Alzheimer's disease or senile dementia is a degenerative disease in which the brain tissue is destroyed, particularly in the learning and memory part. Loss of memory for recent events is often the earliest sign of the disease. As the dementia progresses intellectual deterioration is more marked. Personality changes occur; there is a loss of concentration and carelessness over appearances. The gait becomes unsteady and there is a danger of falls. Incontinence is usually a late symptom of the disease and in extreme cases the individual gradually becomes unable to wash or dress unaided.

There is no satisfactory method of treatment of Alzheimer's disease. The big danger is that treatable conditions such as vitamin deficiency and metabolic disorders may be mistaken for dementia and go untreated.

Behan (1981) estimates that one in 15 people over the age of 65 years will suffer from Alzheimer's disease and that they will live only one-third as long as healthy people. It is three times more common in women than men. There are some instances of family history of the disease, but most cases are sporadic. Most people suffering from dementia either live alone or with their families, yet for every one in institutional care, five elderly people suffering from this disease are cared for at home. There is a role for medication in dementia to relieve symptoms of agitation, sleep disturbance, aggression, over-activity and depression, but such drugs need to be used with caution so as not to increase the confusion and falls.

Dementia is probably the biggest single problem facing the health and social services. It places great stress on the family and the community, is a burden on the economy, overloads general and psychiatric hospital beds, and puts pressure on residential homes and day centres. It is therefore not only humane, but economically prudent, to support the families who look after the elderly and demented person.

'Put Away'

When we think of the elderly and mentally frail, if we think of them at all, it is usually in relation to the problems they cause us, but it would be a sad and slightly unfair world if we did not occasionally stop and think of the problems we cause them.

One of the commonest fears among elderly people is that of being 'put in a home' or 'taken away'. Because of that fear they will sometimes struggle on, afraid to ask for help, in case that denotes dependence and therefore inability to cope. The older person who knows that he or she is getting more forgetful is in even greater fear of being put into 'the asylum'.

"At 94 Mrs D was getting a little deaf, her eyesight was failing, she became confused and forgetful, kept having little 'accidents', and was dependent on a niece to bring her in a bit of shopping once a week, but refused to allow the niece to ask for help because 'they would just want to put her in a home'. Eventually the niece, who was 72 years old herself and suffering with arthritis, felt she could no longer cope and asked me to call on Mrs D.

It's always difficult to call on an elderly person who you know has not requested a visit, does not want you to visit and will probably be frightened or belligerent because you have visited. You need to be fairly sure of your purpose and usefulness before inflicting unnecessary worry or anxiety on people by doing so.

At first she was adamant that she neither wanted or would accept help, then she gradually changed to a tearful 'I can manage to look after myself'. When I told her that it was very expensive to keep people in homes and we would much rather she looked after herself in her own home, she at last agreed to have help. Her memory for recent events was somewhat erratic, but her memory for past events was good. On a subsequent visit, when she no longer thought we wanted to put her away, she told me that she had been born in the workhouse because her father had died and her mother was without support. When she was 16 and in service, she had been 'put in the family way by Himself', and she had found herself back in the workhouse to have the baby. The baby had died some months later and she had been found another kitchen job by 'the Master', although whether that was the workhouse master or 'Himself' I never discovered, but the horror of those days lived on in her memory and it was easy to see why she did not wish to be 'put away' again."

Elderly people fear rejection, particularly by their family and friends, but also by the professionals. The depressed elderly certainly need constant reassurance that people do like them. It is difficult to keep up a continuing flow of reassurance, especially for the family who have to live with them. Most of us have at some time or other suffered from a depression, or sense of loss, but with most of us it is a temporary phase and quickly over. It should, however, give us some idea of how desperate a feeling it is, and therefore give us tolerance.

The elderly fear dependency and loss of control over their lives. If they have to cope with mental illness, they fear our prejudices and exasperation. They fear ridicule, so rather than make mistakes they stop making the effort. In fact, they fear the things we all fear, but they fear them a little more.

The Gaslight Phenomenon

Whitehead (1979) gave this interesting label to a phenomenon with which we are all familiar. He took his title from a play by Patrick Hamilton called 'Gaslight'. Written in 1939, its theme was a plot by a husband to get rid of his wife by having her committed to an asylum as insane. Whitehead described various fraudulent attempts to get rid of people by having them admitted to psychiatric hospitals.

The elderly are, of course, at particular risk here. It's not just the family trying to get rid of Granny because she has become impossible to live with, or the staff of an old people's home trying to get rid of a wandering, quarrelsome resident. It can, as Dr Whitehead points out, be much more sinister than that.

"Mrs Burke was a lady of 70; she had lived alone since the death of her husband a year before. Her son and daughter-in-law suggested that they sell their respective houses and buy a bigger house where they could all live together so that they could give her the care and attention which she needed. When this was done, the new house was put into the son and daughter-in-law's name and soon afterwards Mrs Burke felt that there was increasing pressure being put on her to move out.

She suffered from an anxiety state associated with depression. Her voice had a whining quality which could be very irritating, and she had a highly developed interest in her bowels. She would go to great lengths to explain what medication she had to take, and what position she had to adopt, in order to get her bowels to act in what to her was a reasonable manner. She would then go into great detail as to amount (never enough), colour (varied through the spectrum) and texture of the offending stool, so she was not the easiest of people to live with.

However, the pressure that was being put on her to 'find somewhere else to live', or 'go back to the mental hospital' did not include any repayment of the £20 000 or so that she had paid into the house, and as she had no money left it was not a reasonable suggestion that she find somewhere else to live. All they were doing was to increase her anxiety and deepen her depression.

Mrs Smith was 75 when she married for the second time. Her husband was 10 years her junior, a charming, considerate, thoughtful man. He gradually took over her financial affairs because it seemed senseless to pay an accountant when he was so clever with figures. She became a little confused and his story of her rambling about all night, lighting fires, switching on the gas but forgetting to light it, and refusing to take her tablets sounded so sincere and yet.... . A friend managed to get her son home on a visit from Australia and he took her away for 3 weeks to stay with some friends. Her confusion cleared, and on her return her financial affairs were put back into the accountant's care with very tight control held by the bank. She suffered no further confusion.

Mrs Jones was a very elderly alcoholic, living alone in terrible conditions in a little terraced house. She had become ill from a mixture of starvation and alcoholism. Quite soon after the community nursing staff became involved a 'friend' and her husband moved in to look after the old lady. This charitable act was hailed with delight by all, but very soon the situation was causing concern. It had to be pointed out to the 'friend' that the old lady's bedroom must have some heat, as it was mid-winter; that it was not a good idea to open the window wide even if the smell of urine was at times strong; that the old lady needed food and not brandy. Within 8 weeks the old lady was dead. She probably would have died even if she had been moved to hospital, a move incidentally strongly objected to by both the old lady and the 'friend'. It then turned out that within those 8 weeks the old girl had made a will in favour of the 'friend'."

But it is not only families, friends and neighbours who reject and cheat old people. Rejection is no less destructive when it comes from the professionals. If anything it is more destructive because our reports carry more weight. We are all very quick to call for residential care for our elderly psychiatric patients. It's easier for us to have them off our patch and on to someone else's. Instead of saying, 'How can we help this person to live in the community?' we are much more likely to say 'The risk is too great; they must be removed to a place of safety', which inevitably entails admission to a psychiatric hospital. It is to be hoped that the employment of more community psychiatric nurses will mean more support for people who would otherwise be admitted.

Falling between the Stools

There is a curious 'no man's land' in the health care of the elderly and mentally frail, called, for want of a better name, 'falling between the stools'. The stools in question are the family, the geriatric department, the psychiatric department, the social services department and the primary health care team. An onlooker would be forgiven for thinking that all the aforesaid people were abrogating their responsibility, that they were all doing a Pontius Pilate act of washing their hands of the problem, but in truth it can be a very difficult situation indeed.

The unfortunate person who is doing the falling is elderly, *non compos mentis* and behaving in such a fashion as to disturb the family. The family, quite rightly, go to the general practitioner for help and that is when the merry-go-round starts. It frequently turns out that the 'patient' is too disturbed for the social services department, not disturbed enough for the psychiatric services department, and if disturbed at all is not eligible for the geriatric department, yet cannot be contained within the family unit. Here again, things are brighter in health districts which can call on the expertise of a psychogeriatric department.

It can be soul destroying for the people doing the caring: they may need to keep a 24 hour watch on the patient, and very soon the situation becomes intolerable due to lack of sleep. The family gets bewildered by the number of people who call, go away and send someone else. By the time they have worked their way through the general practitioner, the health visitor, the geriatrician, the social worker and the psychiatrist, tempers and nerves are beginning to fray at what they see as 'buck-passing'.

Even if the psychiatrist, recognising a social as much as a mental need, offers a bed, the 'patient' may well refuse it, and then it becomes difficult to convince the family that one cannot simply take people away. The family may become demanding and aggressive and we unfortunately tend to react with resentment and avoidance. We label them difficult and that mollifies our guilt feelings at our inability to help.

The acute situation resolves itself by either the mental condition becoming worse and necessitating admission on an official order (see below), or the carer becomes physically or mentally exhausted, or the 'patient' damages him/herself physically (fractured femurs are the order of the day) and needs to be admitted to a general hospital. Whatever the circumstances, the family and neighbours at least have the satisfaction of saying 'I told you so'.

The need for a psychogeriatric department in all health districts has now become vital and should become one of the principal political band-wagons of anyone connected with the elderly. There is no doubt that fast, considerate relief given to families under stress pays off. Relatives are happy and willing to care for their elderly mentally as well as physically frail as long as they know that when they need help they will get it.

The Mental Health Act and Compulsory Admission

The Mental Health Act of 1959 repealed all previous Acts. It provides for the compulsory admission of anyone suffering from a mental illness which constitutes a serious danger to the health or life of the patient or the safety of others. The patient can be admitted to any hospital as long as the managers of that hospital are willing to accept them: this invariably means a psychiatric hospital.

Major points regarding the main sections of the Act are given below.

SECTION 29

This section is generally used for urgent or emergency admissions and the detaining period is for 3 days only, the day of admission counting as day one. If it is necessary to detain the patient longer, then Section 25 must be used. Section 29 however, is the one which causes the most concern as being open to misuse, as only one doctor needs to make the recommendation and, although the Act says that it is desirable that he has prior knowledge of the patient, it is not necessary. Application is by the next of kin or the social worker and the recommendation signed by one doctor.

SECTION 25

This section is used to admit a patient for observation and the detaining period is for 28 days. The application is made by the next of kin or the social worker and the recommendation must be signed by two doctors, usually the general practitioner and the psychiatrist. They must have seen the patient within 7 days of each other, and they, and the applicant, must have seen the patient within 14 days of admission.

SECTION 26

This section is an infrequently used section and permits compulsory treatment for up to 12 months. After 6 months, the patient has the right to appeal to the Mental Health. Review Tribunal. Application and medical recommendation are as under Section 25, but would obviously have to be much more detailed.

SECTION 60

This section is concerned with orders made by the court and supported by two medical recommendations for the compulsory treatment of a patient convicted of a criminal offence.

SECTION 136

This section gives the police authority to remove a mentally disturbed person from a public place and take him to a 'place of safety'. Like Section 29, this is valid for 3 days.

According to Pitt (1974) only about 5 per cent of the elderly admitted to hospital because of mental illness are actually admitted under compulsory sections, and fortunately the rest are admitted informally.

(The situation in Scotland is slightly different and in most cases the approval of a Sheriff is necessary to make the order effective.)

Problems of Relatives Caring for the Confused

One of the main problems, apart from the actual caring process, is that relatives do not know who to go to for help. They cope with a gradual deteriorating situation, accepting that the care of 'Mother' or 'Father' is their responsibility, without expecting society to provide. A survey in Edinburgh (Williamson and Stokoe, 1964) found that 80 per cent of the severely or moderately demented people identified were not known to be suffering from this problem by their GP.

Relatives should be told not only the diagnosis, but also the prognosis, so that they know what to expect. At the same time they should be told what help is available to them and to the patient. It is usually only when a crisis situation occurs that the services become involved. The family should have one particular agency that they can go to for help and advice. It does not really matter who that immediate contact is — the GP, the health visitor, the community psychiatric nurse, the district nurse or the social worker. It is important that they have someone they can relate to, someone who will listen, help with the stress, alleviate the problems and reduce the tension.

PRACTICAL HELP AVAILABLE

One of the first things that relatives or those caring for the elderly demented patient should do is bring the situation to the notice of the GP, the health visitor and the local social services department. They should then go on to investigate the availability of financial help such as the Attendance Allowance, and inquire into the possibility of day care, laundry service, short term care for holiday relief, help with incontinence (all discussed more fully in chapter 5) and community psychiatric nursing services. Problem symptoms can probably be relieved by medication from the GP. Night wandering, for instance, can be very destructive to the rest of the family, and yet may easily be relieved by the proper use of night sedation.

It is possible to obtain aids and adaptations to the house which encourage mobility. Voluntary visitors or 'sitters' can allow the relative time to shop. If the elderly person lives alone, they may manage with the assistance of the home help and meals on wheels. But if they can afford it they may be better able to cope by employing a private domestic help who can visit daily and see to their shopping and cooking.

Conclusions

The majority of us have difficulty in dealing with the mentally ill for many reasons, but chief among them must be our ignorance of the whole field of mental health, our irrational fear of violence from the mentally ill, and our embarassment when faced with uninhibited behaviour. We feel more at home with physical illness and shy away from the mentally ill, perhaps in the hope that if we ignore them for long enough they might just go away.

However, the fears of the mentally ill about society are often as strong as are our's of them, and probably with more reason. They fear our ability to decide their life-style. They fear our power to 'put them away', and they are right to do so because it is not always pure humanitarianism that dictates our actions.

We should look closely at our attitudes and be more willing to consider alternatives to residential care for our elderly and mentally frail.

The 1 per cent of the elderly mentally ill in hospital occupy more than half the beds, a fact that should shame us all, because we all are aware that many of them need not be there. Every time it is proposed to open a half-way house for the mentally disturbed within the community there is a scream of horror from all the surrounding householders who insist that it will lower the value of their homes if 'those people are allowed to come and live in the street'.

Unless we, the professionals, alter our attitude, what hope have we got of getting the general public to alter theirs? Our primary concern should be the appointment of a psycho-geriatrician in every health district with proper back-up hospital facilities. Until we get the proper facilities we won't come anywhere near giving the right sort of support to the elderly and mentally frail or their families.

References

Bartlett's Quotations, Macmillan, London.

Behan, P. (1981). Alzheimer's disease. *Medikasset,* **14** (6).

Kay, D. W. K., Beamish, P. and Roth, M. (1964). Old age mental disorders in Newcastle upon Tyne. Part I: A study of prevalence. *British Journal of Psychiatry,* **110**, 146.

Mental Health Act 1959, HMSO, London.

OHE (1979). *Dementia in Old Age,* Office of Health Economics, London.

Pitt, B. (1974). *Psychogeriatrics,* Churchill Livingstone, Edinburgh.

Williamson, J. and Stokoe, I. H. (1964). Old people at home — their unreported needs. *Lancet,* i, 1117.

Whitehead, J. A. (1979). *Psychiatric Disorders in Old Age,* Harvey, Miller and Medcalf, Aylesbury, pp. 15-18.

7 Eccentricity

Introduction

There is an infinite variety about the human race and yet everyone tends, in any one society, to lead similar lives. We dress alike; we eat the same foods; we try to melt into the crowd. We do not, generally, want to draw attention to ourselves. I say generally because there is a small percentage of individuals, in all societies, who dress and behave to please themselves. They are people who don't give a fig for convention and they do not care what society thinks of them. They are what we loosely term 'eccentrics'. The eccentric is found at all levels of society and in all social classes; they lend a lot of colour and humour to life, and many of them are elderly. They are not mentally confused, nor are they disorientated. They may be unconventional, it is true, but they are sociable beings who enjoy life. Included in this group of eccentrics, but within a sub-category of their own, are the hoarders. Hoarders accumulate things until their entire home becomes an enormous collection of jumble. Apart from the obvious social disadvantage of living in overcrowded squalor, the main danger to this group is the risk of fire and infestation from vermin.

The recluses make up another quite separate group. The difference between the eccentrics and the recluses is that the former are happy with people, as long as nobody interferes with their way of life, but the recluses are loners and prefer their own company. The recluse is likely to end up in an unsanitary, pathetic, malnourished state, and is the one who presents the community with its most difficult dilemma — to remove them or not to remove them against their will'.

In this chapter we shall be looking at some of the various

'eccentrics', particularly elderly eccentrics, in society and raising some of the questions they pose to the rest of us. Yet they all have a part to play in the rich kaleidoscope of life. In dealing with them we are dealing with individuals, and this should make us stop and think of them *as individuals* and re-examine our attitudes and motives towards the elderly in general.

The Eccentric

One of the lovely things about working with people in their own homes, especially the elderly, is that one comes to know and appreciate the true eccentric, the person for whom the ordinary rules and regulations don't apply, or if they do apply, the true eccentric will simply ignore them.

"One of the first people I ever visited in my district was a unique character, 'a one-off' as she once referred to herself. Blind and in her 80s, with a badly ulcerated leg, she yet managed to maintain an independent existence. Oh yes, she had home help and meals on wheels and the district nurse to dress her legs, but they were all 'incidental'. What really mattered in her life was her music. She lived in rented accommodation at the back of an antique shop in a two up, two down household. The rooms were barren, devoid of any sentimental knick-knacks. Downstairs the living room and kitchen were strictly utilitarian; upstairs the bedroom was cold and cheerless; the other room was sumptuously adorned with a baby grand piano and a harmonium. Painting and busts of the 'Masters' were everywhere.

One morning, while I was dressing her leg, she told me that she had come from a musical family and that she and her sister had gone to Germany to study music when she was 16. Her love of music took second place to her love for the son of the house, Wilhelm. Unfortunately the clouds of war returned her to England and sent Wilhelm off to die for his Kaiser. But that was not the end of the affair. She and Wilhelm, who she now called 'my little Willie', were in daily contact. He left her a spiritual rose on her breakfast tray every morning and she often played for him in the evening. Nor was he her only visitor. In the evening the 'Masters' all came to play with her, or to listen to her, or to play for her. She called them all by their Christian names and from what she told me they were all very matey and jolly.

One morning the home help had forgotten to bring her some item of shopping and as I had to visit in the near vicinity that evening I said I would buy it and bring it with me on my evening rounds. I had forgotten that blind people do not require lights and, when I returned, I stumbled round in the dark trying to find the light switch, feeling very foolish and inadequate. Even when I found it and switched it on there was not much difference because she only used 40 watt bulbs. Having no need for them herself, she saw no reason to waste her money on bright lights for the use of her infrequent evening visitors.

She was grateful for my little extra visit and as a reward she invited me upstairs to hear her play. Again there was the embarrassment of my stumbling round while she told me where the light switch was and I could feel a sense of panic until I found it and the room was given the benefit of another 40 watt bulb. If anything the situation was a little worse because now there was a dim pool of light in the centre of the big old room and the corners were all in shadow. She walked over to the piano and as she passed the harmonium she smiled and did a little half bow, half curtsy. It was then that my hairs, particularly those on the back of my neck, took on a life of their own. I could feel them rising slowly, while down my back shivers of apprehension and fear contrasted strangely with the beads of perspiration that were running down my face.

'Are, are we a-a-alone, this evening?' I stuttered.

'Oh, we are very honoured, this evening,' she replied, but then she added in an apologetic tone, 'But the Masters will not show themselves while there are strangers in the room.'

'Thank God for that.' I breathed with a sigh of relief.

While she played, and even to my untrained ear it sounded very mediocre, I kept my face averted from the 'Masters' corner' just in case they changed their mind and decided to allow me to join the gang. I don't know if my eyes had got accustomed to the light, but when I left, about

5 minutes later, I got down the stairs, along the hall, out of
the front door and down the alley-way to the main road
quicker than I had ever done it before or ever did again."

Once outside I realised that I had allowed my imagination
to run away with me. A childhood fear of the dark plus a
vivid imagery of ghosts, ghouls and goolies had caught me up
in her daydreams; daydreams, I might add, encouraged by me
over months of visiting in the daylight.

By all the laws of what we tend to think is right for old
people, she should have been in a nice clean home for blind
people, but what a tragedy that would have been for her. No
baby grand piano, no little Willie, no dreams of Liszt, Brahms
and Schumann. Somehow I can't see the 'Masters' visiting in

a home for the blind; the sighted people who look after them need too many lights.

It is not unusual for elderly people, particularly the ladies, to have visitors that nobody else can see. Some of them do carry it to extremes by saving the best chair by the fire or the best seat in front of the telly for their 'visitors'. Occasionally fact and fiction can become so interwoven that it is difficult to sort out which is which, especially if you have come to accept these additions to the household over the years.

"One elderly lady of 80 plus, who lived alone, and it is usually the people who live along who have 'visitors', had a picture of an American Red Indian, complete with feathered head-dress, hanging in her bedroom. This was John, her Guide. If she did not want to do anything then John always advised against it. There was no use arguing with his decision because he carried a lot more clout than we did. It was her way of dealing with our world, the world of professionals who wanted her to eat a better diet, have a warmer house, take up her old cosy mats that she was forever tripping over, accept home help and all the things that she did not want to do. John was her friend and guide and mentor. He told her to tell us to go jump in the lake, politely of course, because she was a very polite old lady."

Sometimes I thought that if I played their game then I might get in on their wavelength, but of course I couldn't. I would find myself talking to the picture with the old lady acting as translator, or listening to her talking to the picture. Either way I would feel a bit foolish, so I would immediately be at a disadvantage. But what a lovely way for a gentle, polite old lady to cope! She did not have to say she would not do what we wanted, all she had to do was smile and say John did not advise it. If she wanted time to think, then she said she would speak to John about it. It was almost like the imaginary friend of childhood, the one who was always responsible for all the naughty things, the one who broke things or left lights on or ate all the biscuits. What would we have done without them?

Eccentrics often go out of their way to draw attention to themselves by wearing clothes which the rest of us would not

be seen dead in. A lovely old man I knew got himself a wonderful collection of brightly coloured hats. A pink hat with an artificial yellow flower stuck in the rim transfigured him from being an ordinary little man into a local character whom people smiled at and passed the time of day with.

These extrovert eccentric people do a great service to the community, especially the elderly, by reminding us that they are individuals with the individual's right to choose their own life-style. If they choose to wear funny clothes, or live what to us are odd lives, they do so because we live in a free society and thankfully they have that choice. They show their independence by flaunting convention and in doing so they remind all of us in the caring professions that, irrespective of age, they are still people. We may think of them as untidy people because they refuse to fit into our little slots; we may find them difficult to cope with because they are not above cocking a snook at the lot of us, but it is their very eccentricity that makes us stop and think. It is the knowledge that not we, nor age, nor society are going to change them that makes us look at them as individuals and should make us look at all the other elderly people about us as individuals too.

The Hoarders

There is probably a bit of the hoarder in most of us. It is a habit that can grow from very small beginnings. There is, however, a difference between being loath to throw things away because they might come in useful some day, and the full-blown collector of their own and everybody else's rubbish. Once you have seen a real hoarder you will come to think of your house as being completely barren.

I once visited a house where a ring at the front door bell brought a sort of disembowelled voice saying, 'Come round the back.'

"Once inside the reason was immediately obvious; the front door had so much stuff piled up against it that it had reached ceiling height. The wonder was that the occupants ever heard the door-bell at all. The living-room had a double bed in one corner on which a man was lying; I never did find out who he was. The floor was at least a foot deep in old clothes and the few chairs in the room were also buried deep in clothes. The lady I had gone to see invited me to sit, but there was truly nothing that I could sit on. As we both looked vaguely round for somewhere, while at the same time balancing precariously on bundles of old clothes, it seemed to strike her that perhaps she was a little overcrowded.

'I'm just having a sort out for the church jumble sale,' she said.

Then there was Miss Jones who had this thing about ash. It was so good for the garden, she said. Such a pity to put it all in the dustbin. Only the winter weather was so cold to keep carrying it out to the back, she said, and anyway she would not be needing it until the spring when she intended to dig it well into the garden. So, in the meanwhile she may as well save it all in the unused dining-room, and in the lounge, and in the front bedroom and in the other three bedrooms. It's amazing how much ash can be collected during the course of one winter from one boiler and one fire.

The difficulty was that she did not always wait for the ash to get cold before adding it to her collection. In the end it got to be a bit of a fire risk and so it had to go. She never forgave us for taking it all away. She could understand us taking a bit, for our own gardens, she said, but to have taken it all, really, you can't trust anyone these days.

'I just won't collect any more for you,' she said, 'if that is how you behave."

What starts as a simple thing with some people can snowball into something of gigantic proportions. Like Miss Jones and her ash and Miss Evans and her paper parcels.

"For years Miss Evans had wrapped things up in paper to keep them clean, all the clean linen, the knives, forks and unused crockery, all nicely wrapped. Then suddenly she started wrapping up the chair and table legs in newspaper to keep them clean. From there she graduated to cupboards, wardrobes and eventually to her own legs. She really did not have many other idiosyncrasies, except that she liked to keep the paper tied on with green garden string. It was not until she got to the electric kettle that the nurses cried halt.

The eccentric and the hoarder are happy with people as long as their life style is undisturbed. If anyone interferes with or tries to alter their way of life or living pattern then they become very annoyed. Eccentrics, however, are not to be mixed up with the recluse; here the pattern of behaviour is different."

The Recluse

Recluses shun friendship and people, and they seem to find it difficult to form relationships. They are loners, and even work colleagues eventually give up trying to get them to join in any sort of activity. When they eventually give up work, and therefore the necessity to keep up some sort of reasonable appearance, they can quickly degenerate into living in slum-like conditions.

There can be few members of the statutory services involved in community work who have not come across a recluse or two. They can be a great trial to neighbours because their gardens become very overgrown, usually into the neighbours' gardens; the house becomes neglected, windows are broken and dividing fences collapse in disrepair. In fairness to the majority of neighbours I have come across, while they abhor the state of the property, it is usually the welfare of the person inside that concerns them most. They wonder 'if she is all right in there?'

A real recluse is usually also a collector of anything and everything imaginable: papers, empty tins, cartons, old clothes. I once found 114 empty baked bean tins in a house and they were the only thing that had been washed in that house for many years — and that included the occupant. They may hoard or they may just accumulate because they can't be bothered to throw things out. A surprising thing is that they are usually intelligent people. Clark (1980) said:

> We found that half the examples studied were from Social Class I and II and had had successful careers. They had enjoyed good upbringing, education and social standing in earlier family life and childhood; evidence of this often remained in the form of antiques and family photographs.
>
> Half showed an intelligence quotient in the highest quarter of the population for their age. Their personalities were normal, with no evidence of neuroses, depression or hysterical tendencies. They did show common features, however, being more aloof and shrewd and less able to form relationships than would be normal. They tend to be rather serious, humourless people with a tendency to distort reality.

I was once asked to visit one of our local recluses by a GP. He had been told by neighbours that they had not seen the old lady for weeks and were getting worried about her. He had called on his morning round and got no answer, which explains why I was standing outside the house at 5 p.m. knocking on all available doors and windows. After about 5 minutes of creating a noise level that, if not sufficient to wake the dead, was at least guaranteed to shake them a little, I could hear movement; slow, hesitant, scraping movement, but someone or something was coming. Eventually the door opened a few inches and the most pathetic scrap of humanity gradually became discernable through the uncombed hair and layers of old rags. She had pushed a chair along the hall until its passage was impeded by the mounds of rubbish and she had then crawled the rest of the way to the door, yet she still spoke with a very delightful voice when she told me it was not very convenient for me to call just at that moment as she was not quite herself.

When I had managed to talk her into letting me in and getting her something to eat, I was able to look about. The roof was leaking and there were odd receptacles placed here and there to catch the water when it rained. There was a very narrow passageway through all the rooms, a bit like Hampton Court maze, with all sorts of stuff piled high on either side. The kitchen was without light other than a candle, and although she had managed to collect three gas cookers only one burner on one cooker was usable. As for the kitchen itself, calling it filthy would have been doing it a great honour. What I would have given for a pair of wellies as I squelched about trying to find food that was not absolutely certain to give her food poisoning. Judging from the amount of mouse droppings about, she shared the house with a very large family of rodents, yet she was oblivious to the idea that the house was at all out of the ordinary.

PROBLEMS FOR THE CARERS

The sadness of the elderly recluse's circumstances is that eventually the need arises for external help, because of illness (which is often due to starvation), or extreme old age, or some form of confusion or cerebral degeneration. Help, which has probably been refused on many previous occasions, will not be readily accepted just because the need is greater. It may then become necessary to force help on an unwilling recipient and this can be a very stressful situation.

It may well be that the home conditions by this time are so deplorable that removal to a place of safety may be the only answer, yet it behoves us all to stop and think who we are doing it for. Are we doing it for the old person's sake? Are we doing it because the neighbours or family are pushing us to 'do something', or are we doing it because these individuals worry us?

PROBLEMS FOR RELATIVES

Relatives find dealing with a recluse a particularly difficult problem. They would dearly like to see 'Aunt Mary' tucked up, nice and clean, in a hospital or home rather than living in sordid, slum-like conditions. One nephew told me, 'I have a permanent guilt feeling about her. I've nagged her so much that she won't even let me into the house anymore.'

Over the years most relatives cease to visit because the recluse has told them to go away so often that they eventually do just that. They cannot understand how a member of the family could wish to live in such terrible conditions. Shame, guilt, anger and exasperation are usual reactions to neighbours and professionals telling them, yet again, that they are concerned for the safety of their relative. One young couple couldn't stand the strain any longer and emigrated to Australia. It is not that the relatives won't help — they are as powerless as everyone else in this situation.

PRESSURES FROM THE COMMUNITY

Sometimes the pressure from the 'authorities' is enough to make elderly people go voluntarily, if not willingly, into hospital or social services accommodation. It is most likely to be hospital in the first instance because of their poor physical condition or incontinence.

One elderly lady had been sitting in an armchair for

several months without moving, being looked after by an equally aged brother. They lived above a shop and it was not until the shopkeeper complained of the 'water' dripping through his ceiling that outside agencies became involved. It took the community nursing staff some weeks to convince not only the patient, but also her brother, that she needed treatment. The landlord giving them notice to quit served as a blessing in disguise because they were rehoused by the council, and we managed to convince her to spend a few weeks in hospital while the move took place.

RESTRAINTS AND THE LAW

If, however, all pleas and suggestions fall on deaf ears, then it may become necessary to resort to compulsory removal under Section 47 of the National Assistance Act 1948. It is never easy to move people against their will; a look at our TV screens when the police are trying to move on demonstrators will indicate how difficult it can be. How much more harrowing it can be to move an old person, probably an ill old person, against their will. It would take a heart of stone not to react to either their demands that their privacy be respected or their cry for pity. Ambulancemen, who are the people usually called upon to carry out the removal, are not renowned for having hearts of stone, or for being indifferent to the odd cry for mercy. An ambulanceman once said to me that he reckoned that the person who applied for the compulsory removal in the first place should be the one to carry it out! I think he had a point.

THE PROFESSIONALS' DILEMMA

The person involved in day to day care of a recluse, be it social worker, district nurse or health visitor, is caught in a cleft stick. The situation deteriorates before your eyes and yet the old person refuses to budge.

"The old lady with the leaking roof was a case in point. Finding her and assessing her needs was easy; solving the problem of what to do with her was anything but easy. Staff from the home care department took one look at the house and said that there was no way they could help to maintain anything, much less anyone, in those conditions. Not that I blamed them; there was no usable heating system in the house and winter was approaching fast. Food, or the absence of it, became a nightmare. The rains came and the pots and pans filled with revolting frequency, helped on by the old dear who found them nearer than the toilet. She spent all her time rolled up in a little ball in the middle of a large double bed covered with a vast collection of old coats, blankets and eiderdowns. Everyone agreed that she would have to be moved and yet I waited, struggling on, hoping she would go willingly.

'Of course, she'll give up and die when she's moved,' said the Jonahs, and secretly I agreed with them.

'She'll die of hypothermia if she stays here,' said others, and it was by now bitterly cold in the house, even fur boots and overcoats made little impression.

I went to the GP, who called in the consultant geriatrician and community physician. They had no more success than I had had in persuading her to go to hospital, but at least there was now the offer of a bed. The community physician then brought a magistrate along and the order for compulsory removal was a matter of formality. It was so cold in the house that the magistrate found it difficult to fill in the form and the fact the he almost walked into one of the bowls of water meant that his stay was not a long one. The ambulancemen came; she was asleep; we woke her gently.

'Come on my love, I've got a nice warm bed and a lovely hot cup of tea waiting for you,' said one of the ambulancemen.

'That will be very nice,' she smiled up at him, while he wrapped her up snug and warm in his blankets and carried her off to the hospital."

Not only did she not die, she took on a new lease of life and lived very happily and contentedly and very well fed in a private rest home for the next 7 years. She eventually died at the ripe old age of 97. So much for my weeks of unnecessary worry, stress and fear that I might be responsible for her shuffling off her mortal coil a bit prematurely. But can we always be sure things will turn out as well and happily? The dilemma of when to interfere with an individual's freedom, to intervene in the interests of the client's welfare, is always hazardous. Whatever is done will bring forth criticism as well as commendation. One just has to wait until one is sure it really is in 'their interest' and not just a way of tucking them away, nice and tidy and out of sight.

LEGAL PROVISIONS

Section 47 of the National Assistance Act 1948 gives appropriate authorities the power to remove people from their home and take them to hospital or residential accommodation which Part III of the same Act says must be provided by the local authorities. An immediate order, lasting for 3 weeks, can be obtained from a magistrate. Green (1980) gives a very clear summary of the application procedure:

(1) The GP refers the matter to the community physician.

(2) If the community physician and the GP agree on a Section 47 removal, they issue a formal certificate.

(3) Formal agreement of accommodation being available is obtained, usually from a consultant in geriatric medicine.

(4) Forms in triplicate are submitted to a magistrate.

(5) If the magistrate approves, he signs the order and authorises a named person to supervise transfer (usually a social worker).

(6) Ambulance transport is arranged and the patient is taken to hospital or to Part III accommodation.

(7) Justification of sectioning and the possibility of revoking the order before the end of the 3 week period is constantly reviewed.

(8) Either the patient agrees to remain for further treatment, or the order is extended by a further application by the community physician to the magistrate.

We should be thankful that it is a measure of our caring society that compulsory removal orders following this sad pattern are seldom used.

Conclusions

It might seem as if the dividing line between the behaviour of the eccentric and the hoarder, the self-imposed isolation of the recluse, and the confusion of the mentally frail, is a very thin one, but generally speaking it is not difficult to separate them according to their fairly recognisable patterns of behaviour.

There are times when the edges become blurred because the recluse may become confused due to physical illness, such as pneumonia, and they are no more immune from the possibility of dementia than the rest of us. A person suffering from a confused state may isolate himself and his living conditions may degenerate into chaos. The hoarder may fill the house with so much rubbish that she becomes isolated because family and friends can no longer tolerate her. But, by listening to the client, family, neighbours, home helps and anyone else involved, one can normally build up a very good history of how long the condition has been present, what the individual was like before, and whether the present crisis has developed suddenly or has built up insidiously over the years.

The house of the recluse will probably be easily recognised from the outside. I drive past one every morning on my way to work — there is a tree in the front garden growing into one of the bedroom windows. Occasionally I ask neighbours if they still see the owner pottering about and they assure me that she and her numerous cats are all scraggy but alive and apparently happy. No doubt the day will come when 'someone will have to do something', but sufficient unto the day; she is alive, she is doing her own thing and she may even *want* the tree to grow into her bedroom window.

It is, I think, unfortunate that we have not got many more eccentrics because they bring colour and enthusiasm to their lives and generally to the lives of those around them. They stamp their individuality and their terms on life and make it work for them rather than accept what society decrees is the norm. They make us look at our own standards when we are obliged to examine theirs and, which I feel is most important of all, they don't conform and just occasionally

they tell us what to do with our questions, our forms, our suggestions and our offers of help — something that is almost certainly very good for us.

In this area, care of the elderly throws up a number of difficult questions. Do we have the right to interfere with another person's life? Do we ever have the right to force unsolicited help on an unwilling recipient, even if we feel that their way of life is a danger to their very existence? Do we sometimes allow ourselves to be pushed into action by the strident voices of family and neighbours? Do we sometimes join the 'something must be done' brigade because the way of life of the individual concerned offends our sensibilities, or are we frightened that if they do die in their squalor that the finger of public opinon may be pointed at us as having neglected our duties.

In the end we can only do our best. Having examined our consciences as to motives, we must then go on and do what we think is right in accordance with our humanitarian and professional ethics, always remembering that to some people dignity and respect are as important as warmth, cleanliness and even food itself.

References

Clark, A. N. G. (1980). Diogenes' syndrome. *Geriatric Medicine*, **10** (2), 65-67.

Green, M. (1980). Compulsory removal. *Geriatric Medicine*, **10** (1), 41-45.

National Assistance Act 1948, HMSO, London.

8   The Dying, the Dead and the Bereaved

Introduction

'I'm not afraid to die. I just don't want to be there when it happens.' This fairly well known quotation by Woody Allen summarizes, I feel, most of our attitudes to death.

One could say that death is a fact of life. There is nothing so sure about life than that it will end for all of us, yet it is a subject that we shy away from; it is taboo, proscribed, *verboten*. When people talk about making their wills or putting their affairs in order, there is sure to be someone around to accuse them of being morbid.

Age has a great deal to do with attitudes to death. We are saddened by the death of a child, shocked by the death of a young mother or father, but resigned to the death of an old person. The elderly themselves are usually much more composed about their inevitable demise than we give them credit for. They have watched their friends and contemporaries die and they develop a greater serenity and equanimity about it. What they do want to do occasionally is to talk about it. Unfortunately we do not have that composure; death is still our enemy, we cannot speak of death without looking at our own mortality and so when they want to talk we brush them off with inane remarks such as 'Now don't be silly, you are not going to die.' It's ludicrous really because most old people have come to accept that there is a time for living and a time for dying — it's we who can't accept it.

So, in this chapter an attempt is made to look at death and dying in a rational way. Also discussed are the knotty subjects of suicide, euthanasia, bereavement, grief, the coroner and sudden death, and the practicalities of death, including its cost.

The Dying

Mother Jones, for that was what they called her, had had nine children. Now at the fine age of 95 years, having out-lived five of her children, she was dying. She had lived with one of her daughters for the previous 20 years, ever since her husband had died. So to all intents and purposes she was dying in her own home. The previous day she had gone to bed in the afternoon — an unheard of self-indulgence for the old matriarch.

When her daughter had gone up at tea time to find out if she was getting up, the old lady was sitting bolt upright in bed, finding great difficulty in breathing and with a pale rather clammy appearance.

'You've caught a chill, Mother, I'll call the doctor,' she said.

'Don't bother,' said the old lady, 'I'm dying, you had better send for the Priest.'

'Oh no, Mother, I'll get Dr McCann.'

'Don't be silly, girl, I ought to know if I'm dying,' gasped the old lady, 'Besides, I've just seen your father.'

Despite the fact that Mr Jones had been dead for 20 years, the daughter did not for a moment disbelieve her mother. If her father was indeed around, then it could only be for the express purpose of collecting his wife. They got the priest and the doctor. Neither visit was very private. The old girl had a booming sort of voice that even apnoea could not diminish.

'Do you think I'll get to Heaven?' she joked with the priest.

'I don't think St Peter himself would have the nerve not to let you in,' he replied.

'My Joe called, he'll be back soon.' She sat there getting older and frailer by the minute. Her breathing became more difficult. She slept most of the time. Her family began arriving from all over the country.

'There's not much you can do,' she told the doctor, 'except give the certificate, and I'm not dead yet.'

'Oh yes there is. I can drink some of your fine malt whisky,' he replied. It was a long standing joke with them. They had a great respect for each other.

Her daughter told the rest.

'We were in the room, my sister and I, sitting by her bed. I was holding her hand. My brother and his two sons came upstairs and stood in the doorway; they were talking about picking another relative up from the station. Suddenly, my mother opened her eyes, smiled at me and made as if to pat my hand. Then she looked at the door and said to my brother, "Move over and let you father in." My poor brother almost died of fright, and he certainly moved. But I'll never forget my mother's face. It was so beautiful and peaceful. And she smiled. Oh, I'll never forget that smile. She went to sleep then and about two hours later she died in her sleep without regaining consciousness. It was just three days in all from the time she went to bed. I could not be sad for her. It was her time and she wanted to go to my father.'

A good death. To die surrounded by your family, by those who you have cared for, and who now, in turn, care for you. Members of the health professions have all seen people die, seeing good deaths and sad deaths, and being party to many indifferent deaths. On our 'hurry up and get the work done' wards, we have had people die clean, but alone. The last, but most poignant courtesy that we are able to show to our fellow human beings is to hold their hand while they pass through and out of this world.

Mr Richards was 66 years of age, terminally ill with cancer of the bowel and now with bone secondaries. He had been through the operative and deep ray therapy and had now come home to die. As is fairly usual in these cases, all the discussions about his condition had been entered into when he was not present. Nobody had had the politeness or good manners to include him. All we had done was burden his wife with the knowledge and make her a party to the inevitable burlesque tragedy that always follows.

'Am I dying? Do I have cancer? Will I get better? Why is my pain getting worse?'

The questions only led to more evasions, more fabrication. His wife was by then unable to withdraw all the falsity; the rest of us in the community caring team justified our reticence by saying it was for Mr Richards' sake. The truth was none of us had the courage or the ability to let him tell us what he knew.

Saunders (1965) says, 'The real question is not "What do you tell your patients?" but rather, "what do you let your patients tell you?" Learn to hear what they are saying, what is hidden underneath, what is going on.'

Mr Richards fairly quickly got to the stage of needing intensive nursing care and pain control and he had the good fortune to be admitted to a local hospice. Even then we were all very careful to refer to it as a nursing home with special expertise. I happened to be in the hospice the next day and called into his ward to see him. He was very angry. Angry with me, angry with his doctor and with his wife. For the first time someone had had the honesty and the courage to tell him the truth and his anger was not directed at fate for choosing him to die, it was directed at us for lying to him and depriving him of the right to sort things out.

'Why didn't you tell me the truth? God knows I asked

often enough,' he demanded.

'Because I didn't have the courage,' I replied.

'What courage does it take on your part? I'm the one going to die.'

'Not everyone wants to know and it's difficult once the evasion starts to find the right moment to say it.'

Even as I made all the excuses I knew how stupid and futile they sounded.

'They found the right moment here easily enough, I can't accept that none of you could not have done so long ago. And my wife', he went on, 'How could Doris have lied to me all the time?"

'You can't blame her. Most wives start off by not believing the diagnosis themselves. Then they go through the hoping for a miracle stage and by the time they do accept it, it is too late. The denial, the lies, have all been going on for too long.'

I was glad that I was his first visitor after he had been told his diagnosis. He had a need to lash out at someone and rather me than his wife. In a way it was almost like reparation for my omissions. His anger was so justified and so right. The hospice asked Mrs Richards to see the Medical Director before she saw her husband later that day. I thought she in turn might be angry that he had been told, but all she felt was a great relief that the barrier had been removed. They fell into each others arms and wept and hugged and talked and talked and talked.

Why is it that so few of us can talk of death to the dying? Is it because we are embarrassed by failure? After all, this is one that is going to get away, one we have failed to cure, and we are processed to cure, not to fail. Or is it that we are afraid of the emotions we might unleash if we were to tell the truth? Is it that we are fightened to look at our own mortality?

It is not always a nurse's prerogative to decide if or when a patient should be told, but it is very much within the nurse's duty to listen to the patient and to inform the doctor of her feelings and insights. It is also our right as relatives to be consulted by the medical profession if near members of our family are incurable. Not that it is ever an easy or clear-cut decision. Many doctors believe it to be against the patient's best interest to tell him — or is it really that? Could it be that they use this as a convenient cover for their natural embarrassment. The British 'stiff upper lip' syndrome. 'Big boys don't cry' and if you tell them they are dying they might just forget their stiff upper lip and break down and weep all over you.

WHERE DO PEOPLE DIE?

Doyle (1980) says that about 70 per cent of people now die in hospitals, nursing homes or hospices. On the other hand, Agate (1979) says, 'The fact is that most deaths still do take place at home, and home nurses and doctors devotedly see the matter through with courageous, helpful friends.' The real answer probably lies somewhere between, depending on what part of the country you live in, and what the local ethos on death is.

Given the option, I'm sure most of us would choose to die in the bosom of our family. If we can't have that, the next best thing is to die in a hospice where the staff are dedicated and enlightened enough to care totally and where they will talk to us and allow us to talk to them. I should think the worst possible form of dying would be to have to do it alone, either at home, or in a nice hospital ward, tucked away in the end bed behind closed curtains.

Perhaps in the end the best thing we can do for the dying is to listen to them, to be honest with them and to accept the fact that they have inalienable rights. The right to know, the right to be involved in their treatment, the right to decide whether that treatment is appropriate for them, and the right to decline treatment.

THE DYING AND THEIR FAMILIES

Anyone who has watched families care for their dying will know that it is never an easy task. It can, however, be a rewarding task, particularly in the care of an elderly relative. There are two obvious reasons why the strain sometimes becomes too great: (1) the lack of sleep and sheer physical tiredness on the part of the caring members and (2) their concern that the dying member is in pain or discomfort which they cannot relieve. These are areas in which the professional members of the primary health care team and the social services department can give so much help and support. If we can contain the situation within the home and allow the elderly relative to die there, the sense of achievement and satisfaction felt by the family will go a long way towards helping them to come to terms with the death.

The guilt felt by some families, who allow their elderly Mum or Dad to be 'taken away', particularly if they have cared for someone through weeks or months, only to allow them to go days and sometimes hours before they die, is especially distressing. I've known people still feeling sad and guilt-ridden about it 20 years later: 'I cared for him right up to the end, but he died in hospital. I wish I'd never let him go.'

Mrs Parsons was a 79 year old, caring for her 83 year old husband who had had a stroke some 5 months previously. How she ever managed to get him in and out of bed on to the commode I'll never know, but she did, and what's more, she did it willingly and lovingly.

When I spoke to her about the Attendance Allowance, she said they had never had anything from the social people. Fred would not have liked that; they had always managed on their pensions. I explained that this was an allowance given to people who needed full time care and she replied, 'But I don't need to be paid to look after my Fred.'

Eventually, with a little more explanation and encouragement she filled in the form. A month or so later, when she had had a week of broken nights and was looking very tired and frail, she accepted the suggestion that she have a little rest and that Mr Parsons should go into hospital for a short stay of 2 weeks. Even then she spent every afternoon in the ward holding his hand but at least her nights were restful. Unfortunately, just before he was due to come home he had another stroke and died. I don't think she will ever forgive herself. It is the one thing that blots her memory of him and their life together. We gave her a few nights sleep and the rest of her life to regret it.

Many sons and daughters show great responsibility and devotion towards their ageing, infirm or disabled parents. Many give up their careers to care full time for parents, and many others who cannot afford to stop work take on the dual roles of care and work. During the terminal stage of an illness the carer can become physically and mentally exhausted. The joy and satisfaction of caring for mother or father until the end can be marred by the feeling of irritation and annoyance brought on by tiredness. If we can look after the carer properly they will then gain strength and satisfaction afterwards to help cope with the inevitable grief of bereavement.

Sudden Death and the Duties of the Coroner

A coroner may be a solicitor or a doctor. It is not usual to find full time officials holding qualifications in both law and medicine. The majority of coroners are part time officers and they are appointed for a stated area or district. The coroner is informed when there is a violent or sudden death, if the cause of death is unknown, or if the deceased has not been seen by a doctor immediately after death or within 14 days before death. Doctors will normally inform the coroner if they have any doubts about the circumstances of a death, but it is the Registrar who has the legal responsibility of informing the coroner of anything other than normal certification.

It is the coroner who will decide if a post-mortem examination of the body is to be carried out. If he requests a post-mortem, then on receipt of the pathologist's report it is his decision whether an inquest will be held. He has legal obligations towards certain types of sudden death and he must hold an inquest if the death has been due to unnatural causes.

The purpose of an inquest is to find out the identity of the deceased, how, where and when the death took place, and if anyone is to be charged with causing the death. Once the case is referred to the coroner the body may not be disposed of without his permission.

Bereavement

A man's dying is more the survivors' affair than his own

Thomas Mann (1924)

Elderly people accept the prospect of their own death. What they find very hard to accept is the death of their partners: 'We always prayed we could go together.' The death of their husband or wife is a crisis of loss as deep and as crippling as the loss of a leg or an arm. The pain, the shock, the feeling of being incomplete are as acute as a physical pain, but there is no outward appearance of disability. The bereaved do not always get the same sympathy or consolation as the physically injured.

For the young or middle-aged, the death of a partner can be an emotionally devastating experience but with time the scars can heal and there is a chance of a second marriage or relationship. If you are 80 or more and you lose your partner, it is unlikely that there is going to be another bite at the cherry, so losing is for ever. No matter how long the illness was, or how hard or arduous the work of looking after the ill person was, the sense of loss will be completely catastrophic. If the death has taken place in hospital, there can be a strong sense of guilt that the bereaved could not look after him/her themselves.

'The nurses did their best but they were always so busy' and 'The doctors never seemed to have time to tell us what was happening' are commonly stated attitudes expressed by bereaved elderly people whose husbands or wives have died in hospital.

Grief is the normal reaction to loss. Morrice (1976) says,

Grief may be defined as the emotional and physical reaction to any important personal loss. It is in fact normal and appropriate in such circumstances. Grieving, if completed successfully, brings psychological acceptance of the loss and the restoration of emotional equilibrium.

We must, then grieve before we can come to terms with our crisis of loss. There are two principal stages in any crisis and the crisis of bereavement has a very acute stage which includes shock, disbelief, anger, and blaming, either oneself or others. This is followed by a period of numbness, lethargy and depression. Weeping is common and often uncontrolled. Physical symptoms and pains apeing the pain of the dead partner can be distressing; insomnia, anorexia and the feeling of being incomplete is frequent. The newly bereaved person is constantly saying 'We' instead of 'I'. They hear something interesting or amusing and immediately think, 'I must tell George that', only to realise almost at once that George is no longer there to tell.

Realisation brings wretchedness and tears. The person who a minute ago was smiling is suddenly standing there with tears running down their cheek. This unfortunately makes most people feel very inadequate and uncomfortable, and their way of coping with the bereaved is to keep away from them. We accept their need to mourn. Indeed, we tell them that they need to mourn and grieve in order to work through their loss, then we try and avoid them in case we become involved in the mourning process. After a while, many of us treat bereaved people as if they were indulging themselves by wallowing in grief. We have all met, and unfortunately most of us have used, the old, 'Well, now, that's all in the past, we must pull ourselves together' bit.

RESOLUTION OF THE CRISIS OF BEREAVEMENT

There is no magic time or moment when one can say, 'My grieving is over'. However, one cannot continue to feel grief-stricken forever. Life does return to something approaching normality. Gradually the tension eases, although there will be periods of remembrance and depression. Anniversaries, birthdays and special days will bring renewed sorrow at first. But, out of all adversity can come strength. The knowledge that one has learned to cope with one's grief and that one can do all the things which the partner usually did is gratifying. Life can and will go on.

Mrs Simmons was only 65 when her husband died. He had been 10 years older than her so she had expected him to die before her, but not so soon. The house which they lived in belonged to her late husband's family, and as soon as the funeral was over pressure was exerted on Mrs Simmons to vacate the house. She knew she had some tenancy rights, and the family always prefaced their enquiries with the fact that they would not put her out in the street, but the pressure, nevertheless, was very real: 'How are you? Have you managed to find anything yet? You know we would never put you out, dear, but money is very tight with us, and we would like to sell the house.'

This sort of arm-twisting, on top of bereavement, caused Mrs Simmons to come very near to a breakdown. Her anxiety caused her to talk non-stop. I've never known a woman to talk so much. She would telephone every day and give any-one who would listen a resume of the previous 24 hours. We managed to get her a flatlet in a housing association block, and the telephone calls increased because now there were frequent decisions as to what piece of furniture to take and what to sell. Eventually she moved in and all the other tenants were included in her chatter. People moved away as fast as they could when they saw her coming. The care-taker of the block said she could empty the lounge faster than a mad dog. Attempts at voluntary work were unsuccess-ful and unsatisfactory. We staggered from one situation to another.

About 6 months later, Mrs Simmons came to see us. The difference was unbelievable. She was very well dressed and groomed and almost silent. She described her experience in terms of having gone through a tunnel of grief and come out the other end into the sunshine again. She said, 'I know I'm better now because I don't dream about the tunnel anymore. I could always see a light at the end of the tunnel, but some-times it was only a little glimmer and at other times it looked quite bright. I wondered if I was going mad, but I know the worst is over now, and I really would like to do something worthwhile'.

Mrs Simmons had talked her way out of her crisis. People do generally have a need to talk. Fortunately not all of them are as loquacious as Mrs Simmons, but the need to talk about their bereavement, the need to rationalise the loss, is common to us all. We have a compulsion to go through the

'Why me?' 'What have I done to deserve this?' series of questions as part of the natural anger of the crisis.

The elderly in particular have this need to talk, and we do our best service to them by just listening, by letting them retell us the same story — 20 times if necessary. Listening is much more difficult than feeding them antidepressants, but it works better. The dilemma of bereavement is that we will treat it as an illness and be too ready to offer the night sedation and the antidepressants and that we will fail to see that the crisis is not being resolved and that the bereaved person is becoming seriously depressed.

✗ The abnormal or pathological continuation of grief is a closed area to most of us. Unless we have experienced a bereavement ourselves, we have little training in this field. There is a suggestion that with the decline in the traditional support of organised religion, and therefore less support from the clergy in times of death and bereavement, increasingly this function will be seen as a duty of the caring professions. It is important that we do not encourage the bereaved to see themselves as sick. We all have to cope with loss, of job or status and through divorce or death. The crisis process can be a long one, but most of us, with help, can cope in time, and some of us can be strengthened by the coping.

CRUSE

'Cruse' is a voluntary organisation to help the bereaved. It was founded in 1959 by Margaret Torrie. The name is taken from the story in the Old Testament of the widow who shared her meal with a hungry stranger and was rewarded by having her barrel of meal and cruse of oil continually replenished.

The aim of Cruse is to help the bereaved in a practical way. To be used as a bridge, not as a crutch. There are now over 60 branches of the organisation. They also run counselling courses for people working with the dying and bereaved. The local Citizens Advice Bureau will always know of the nearest local branch.

Suicide

LEGAL AND RELIGIOUS SITUATIONS

Since the Suicide Act 1961, suicide has ceased to be a crime. However, it is still a crime to assist others to commit suicide and the courts can impose a penalty of up to 14 years imprisonment. Before 1961, suicide, like homicide, was a criminal offence — the killing with intent of oneself. As late as 1955 a man was sentenced to prison for attempted suicide.

Suicide is still condemned by most religions, which nevertheless have always accepted and loudly acclaimed self-destruction by martyrs for the faith. In the Middle Ages a suicide was not allowed a church funeral, nor was the body allowed to be buried on consecrated ground. Up to 1870 the property of a suicide could be confiscated by the state. There were also many fears about the dead body itself, a mixture of horror, pagan beliefs and religious folklore which resulted in the body being buried at the cross-roads with a stake driven through the heart and a stone at the head. The last such burial took place in 1823.

PRESENT SITUATION

Statistics on suicide are of doubtful pedigree. Coroners are unwilling to record a death as a suicide if there is any doubt, in order to save the relatives. The person intent on committing suicide may be careful not to leave a note for the same reason — the relative or person finding the body may remove a last letter or interfere with the evidence, again so as to save embarrassment.

Many so-called accidental deaths may in fact be suicides. Some car accidents and shotgun accidents have about them an aura of the 'did he fall or was he pushed' quality. While there can be little doubt about the person who jumps off a chair having first tied a noose round his neck, there may well be considerable doubt about the drug overdose.

Like the religions, society views suicide in different ways. If a man gives his life for a cause, whether it be the monks in Vietnam who poured petrol over themselves and then turned themselves into human torches in protest, or hunger strikers who fast until death, or the classic case of Captain Oates going out into the blizzard to die, these altruistic suicides have about them a certain grandeur. In contrast, there is nothing grand or even dignified about the majority of the run of the mill suicides. In fact they tend to be rather messy, and society tends to be uncomfortable and therefore disapproving.

We are almost invariably horrified when we hear that friends and colleagues have taken their own lives. It makes us feel ill at ease and discomforted because we did not see their distress. Because they disturb us we tend to feel annoyed with them: 'Why couldn't they have asked for help?' Although most of us have had periods in our lives when we have felt 'down', it is difficult for us to conceive of a situation in which we could actually end our lives. It is one of the reasons why we are always happy to accept the verdict that they did it while of 'unsound mind' or 'while the balance of their mind was disturbed'.

Fortunately attitudes have changed, in that we are now more likely to pity than condemn, and we know that many attempted suicides are calls for help, not oblivion. On the other hand, we still do have a moral or ethical distaste for the waste of life. Perhaps the puritan in us agrees with those old stalwarts Thomas Aquinas and St Augustine: ' "Thou shall not kill" refers to the killing of a man; not another man; therefore not even thyself. For he who kills himself kills nothing else than a man.' So said St Augustine (354-430).

SUICIDE AND THE ELDERLY

Whitehead (1974) says, 'Old people who are depressed do commit suicide and, in fact, the elderly are one of the high risk groups.' Occasionally you come across elderly people who, in depression, 'turn their backs to the wall'. It can be seen in the close deaths of two old people who have lived together for 40, 50 and sometimes 60 years. When one dies suddenly from natural causes, the other one, within a matter of months will let go of life.

An example of such a case was that of Mrs Rogers, a widow aged 76 years. She had surgery for cancer of the jaw at the age of 73 with a very good recovery. She lived an independent and enjoyable life in the little flat. She had many friends and was very involved with the local church groups. About 6 months after her 76th birthday she became depressed, complained of feeling unwell, stopped eating very much and generally did not look well. Examination showed no recurrence of the cancerous growth, yet she continued to deteriorate. She ate less and less and refused to take medication for the depression.

Then she started to pack up all her belongings and tidy all the cupboards. This done, she asked to be admitted to a nursing home. The admission was taken as a good sign; obviously she felt she needed treatment and would now cooperate. Not a bit of it. She was within 2 months of her 77th birthday and as it got nearer she became more and more agitated. Finally she admitted to her fear. Some 25 years previously a fortune teller had said she would die before her 77th birthday and, as some other predictions of the fortune teller had come true, she believed this one would as well. She had got to the stage of going to sleep each night believing it would be her last and waking up each morning knowing she had to go through the same terrible dread yet again. By now permanent death was preferable to the endless living death she was experiencing. She died a week later.

Old people do end their lives. Most of them have enough drugs in the house not only to take their own lives but to take half the street with them as well. Not many of them are like Mrs Rogers; their depression is usually due to loneliness and despair. It is a recurring theme in this book that simply treating the elderly for the immediate problems of depression will not be of great value unless the cure includes help with their position of isolation from the community.

Elderly people also use suicide as a threat to relatives. Mrs Smyth, an 80 year old widow, was grieving for her third husband, an alcoholic, who had recently died.

'I don't get much sleep but then I have not slept very well since I married John. He used to get drunk every night and he would swear at me to get out of his sight and go to bed. But I could not sleep because he used to smoke. Many a night he fell asleep with the cigarette still alight. He burnt the carpets and the settee and I can't tell you how often he burnt his clothes. My son — I've only got the one — he calls most nights on his way home from work. My daughter-in-law never comes, she's hard, ever so hard, not like my son. I've got two grandsons and one granddaughter, they never come near me, just like their mother. I go to my son's every Sunday for dinner. Sometimes he has to go away and then I don't go. If he doesn't come for a few nights I ring him up to see if they are coming. I sometimes say, " I may as well do away with myself if nobody wants me." I wouldn't ever do it of course . . . '

That's a long way from the real depressed elderly person who weeps easily and admits depression and thoughts of suicide. These are people who need expert help and need it fairly fast. They also need the social and community help equally urgently. They need to know that we care.

Euthanasia

The debate on euthanasia, which the *Concise Oxford English Dictionary* defines as 'gentle and easy death', has been with us in its modern form since the early 1930s. It has had many famous protagonists and antagonists since the English Euthanasia Society was formed in 1935 — to be quickly followed by the American Euthanasia Society in 1938. The aim of the English society was

> To create a public opinion favourable to the view that an adult person suffering severely from a fatal illness, for which no cure is known, should be entitled by law to the mercy of a painless death if and when that is his expressed wish, and to promote this legislation (Trowell, 1973).

The Nazi regime, prior to and during the second world war, practised their own form of euthanasia: it did nothing to further the cause of the societies. The Nazi 'euthanasia programme' did not confine itself to the destruction of the unfortunate Jewish population but included the senile and severely handicapped, both children and adults. Before we allow our thoughts to become too scandalized and nauseated let us never forget that doctors and nurses were involved in the Führer's master plan. It is a revolting and shameful thing that many of them were willing to co-operate in such a programme.

The controversy continues. The moral, ethical, legal and religious aspects of this subject are likely to be debated for a long time. 'Thou shalt not kill' versus 'Death with dignity'. Euphemisms abound: mercy killing, a fair and easy passage, the thin end of the wedge, the right to die, etc. However, the crucial question seems to be, now as always, 'Who does the deed?'

THE LEGAL, MORAL AND RELIGIOUS ASPECTS OF
EUTHANASIA

The doctor and nurse's attitudes are controlled by their
professional ethics as much as by their legal and religious
duties. The churches are all but unanimous on the question
of euthanasia. 'Thou shalt not kill,' and in small print, 'but
thou needst not strive officiously to keep alive,' whatever
that means; there is no doubt that it would mean different
things to different people.

According to Martin (1980),

> The law is clear. Any act intended to bring about the
> death of another is illegal and if death results, a charge
> of murder, with its mandatory life sentence could follow.
> In fact, Judges approach mercy killing cases with a con-
> siderable measure of sympathy and it is not unusual to
> find the charge reduced to one of manslaughter on the
> grounds of dimished responsibility.

Can one legislate for a quiet and painless death? Would a
change in the law really produce the death with dignity that
the Euthanasia Society so fervently advocates? In the end
surely it depends on the attitudes of the family and the
caring professions as to how peaceful a death is.

Morally it can be a difficult and painful thing to sit on the
horns of this particular dilemma. Do you actively resuscitate
the elderly demented patient who has pneumonia, knowing
that the family have already had several years of appalling
strain. Then there is the point made by Kamisar (1978),
speaking of the possible expansion of euthanasia to include
those who become a nuisance to society, such as the senile
and demented:

> I see the issue, then, as the need for voluntary euthanasia
> versus (1) the incident of mistake and abuse; and (2) the
> danger that legal machinery initially designed to kill those
> who are a nuisance to themselves may someday engulf
> those who are a nuisance to others.

The old problems remain. Could safeguards ever be safe enough? Who would administer euthanasia? At what stage of the terminal illness should it be administered? Who would or could decide that the moment had arrived? The right to die or the right to kill?

The medical and nursing professions have come out strongly against voluntary euthanasia, although there are many individuals within them who undoubtedly agree with the Societies. Everyone would agree that death should be as peaceful, painless and dignified as it is humanly possible to make it. Already there is a slight decrease in the number of doctors who feel morally obliged to rush in with the antibiotics to fight the elderly's best old friend — pneumonia.

With care, compassion and an extension of the hospice movement, it might be possible to remove the need for voluntary euthanasia. One would like to think so, but until that time comes the battle will continue. If the end product is that we are made more aware of our responsibilities towards others in their terminal illness, then long may the battle continue.

The Practicalities of Death

Most of us are unfamiliar with what actually happens after a person dies. If asked by the relations we tend to murmur something about getting the death certificate from the doctor and leave it at that. The doctor does not, in fact, issue a death certificate. It is given by the Registrar. There are legal requirements to be met. All deaths must be notified to the local Registrar of Births, Marriages and Deaths within 5 days in England and Wales and within 8 days in Scotland.

When someone dies, a medical certificate showing cause of death is given by the attending doctor. This is taken to the Registrar who in turn will issue (1) a certificate of disposal, which gives the undertaker authority for burial or cremation, and (2) the death certificate. It is as well at this stage to ask for extra copies, for which a small charge is made.

CREMATION

If the body is to be cremated a more detailed form has to be completed. The form is signed by the executor or the nearest relative and countersigned by a witness as to the signatory's identity. The medical certificate must be signed by two doctors, and as this is an extra item of service, a fee will be charged by both. The certificates are carefully examined by yet another doctor; this is the medical referee of the crematorium. This may sound a complicated procedure but it is not as difficult as all that and the modern funeral service includes help with all the forms.

THE UNDERTAKER

Today the service offered by the undertaker or funeral director, as he is far more likely to be called, is all embracing. They supply the know-how and the facilities to negotiate the unitiated through all the complexities of the system. They usually see to all the fees and these are then added to their final bill. Fees may include those to the vicar for his service and for the church if there is a church service; they will also include those of the gravediggers, cemetary or cremation and, of course, his own.

Dying is an expensive business and it is as well to ask just how much it is all going to cost before committing yourself (or more probably your relatives) to a costly extravagance! A simple burial or cremation will cost in the region of £350 to £500 at 1981 prices. Embalming, transport out of the area, opening a new grave, certainly in the London area, can add hundreds of pounds to the cost.

DUTY OF THE LOCAL AUTHORITY

The district, borough or county council has a duty to bury the dead if there are no relatives or finances available. They have the right to reclaim any expense which they can from the estate of the deceased and to claim the death grant towards the costs. In the old days this was known as 'a pauper's funeral', and even now elderly people will cling on to their 'funeral money', whatever they have to do without, in order to avoid the stigma of 'the pauper's grave'.

Although a funeral organised by a local authority is obviously not an elaborate affair, it is the very same service as the simple burial or cremation offered by the funeral directors to the fee-paying clients. It is the local undertakers who perform the function and they tender for this contract with the local authority as any business tenders for contracts. Under certain circumstances the DHSS (Supplementary Benefit Section) will help towards costs.

EMBALMING

Embalming is something that is very popular in the United States. Speaking of the American embalming industry, Jones (1967) says,

> Today embalming is routine in America and there are hundreds of arterial and cavity fluids, eye-caps, tissue builders, which will 'add as much as 20 lbs to the appearance of the body', sure-closes, feature-forms, electric injectors, creams, waxes, surface restorers, sealers, emollient dyes, and liquid cream cosmetics in a long range of colours from suntan through beige to moonlit blond, so that every subject of care can look twenty years younger.

It would rather depend on how much of this particular service you use as to the eventual cost, but in order not to get in too far it would be as well to discuss the cost as part of all the financial details with the funeral people first.

Death inevitably involves rituals, although they are by no means as elaborate as they were 20 years ago. One seldom, these days, hears of a 'wake', except in some rural parts of Ireland or France. The old habit of watching or 'waking' the dead arose partly from a fear of burying someone alive. Some of the implements of death have remained from olden times — the winding sheet or shroud; the sarcophagus or coffin; the memorials to the dead from pyramids to gravestones — but with cremation they have less significance. Even the cremation urn is less likely to be used as ashes are more often than not scattered in the garden of remembrance.

It would seem that while our American cousins go in for embalming we British are not very interested in the beautification aspect. Their funerals get more elaborate while ours get more abbreviated. In America, viewing the body is a widespread custom, and so the deceased must be made socially presentable for their last public appearance. According to Pine (1975), 92 per cent of people who die in America are buried and only 5 per cent cremated. In England, cremation is the method of choice: 60 per cent cremation compared to 40 per cent burial. The custom has probably grown from the shortage of space which has restricted the expansion of existing graveyards and the creation of new ones.

Whatever our reasons, we are continually reducing our customary rituals concerning death. Unfortunately, in doing so we also reduce our outlets for grieving. At the end of our quick funeral trip to the crematorium we leave the bereaved next of kin bereft and alone.

Conclusion

> Death where is thy sting?
> Sans eyes, sans teeth, sans everything.

We have shrouded the whole process of death and dying in such mystery and repugnance that we should not be surprised if the bereaved find it difficult to resolve their crisis or accept their loss. If more bereaved people are going through abnormal crises, it may be because we have removed, in large measure, the comfort of the religious acceptance of death prior to everlasting life in the next world. In its place we now have a secular void.

We are continually reducing the period of mourning and the rituals involved with it to a stage when it is not even considered good manners to talk about death. When our elderly friends or relatives talk about their inevitable demise, instead of hushing them up with pointless remarks we should be encouraging them to state their wishes and to ask if their next of kin or executor knows about their wishes, and where such important items as the insurance policies and bank and savings books are.

Elderly people not only need to talk about these things, but some of them actually enjoy the prospect of arranging their funerals. They were brought up in an age when death was not so taboo and when saving for the funeral was part of every household expenditure. Their fear is always that of having a pauper's funeral, or being buried in the pauper's plot. The one thing that is not allowed in a funeral organised by the local authority is the placing of a headstone on the grave, because, of course, the grave will be used many times over.

Nowadays many of the old penny and shilling insurance policies taken out by the elderly in earlier days will not cover the cost of the modern funeral. The very basic cremation will cost £350 to £400 at 1981 prices. A memorial stone will add another £150 at least. Moving the body from one part of the country to another can add enormously to the bill. Beside all this the death grant of £30 seems quite ridiculous.

Where we die and how we die is of supreme importance to us all. Given the choice, is there anyone who would not wish to die at home among their family? And given the choice, would we really like to be kept in ignorance of our condition if it were considered terminal? Would we not want to know, so that we could at least sort things out and take leave of our friends and family? But to die at home involves the family, and they need and deserve all the help and support we can give them. They too need a chance to talk. In fact, to develop a listening skill is one of the hardest for people who are normally 'doers', but it is one of the paramount skills in any walk of life, and especially in dealing with the elderly.

If left alone after bereavement the elderly can be a suicide risk. Depression, loneliness and isolation add to that risk. Occasionally they may use the word suicide as a threat to relatives, but we should never ignore that threat because it shows that they feel neglected.

Attitudes have fortunately changed towards the attempted suicide in that legal sanctions have been removed and we do, at least, recognise it as a call for help. However, neither legal sanctions nor general attitudes have altered in respect to euthanasia. The euthanasia societies have not managed to alter the view of the caring professions towards voluntary euthanasia. Neither have they yet managed to change the law. It is a subject that will certainly go on being debated, but for the moment the commandment holds: 'Thou shalt not kill.'

References

Agate, J. (1979). *Geriatrics for Nurses and Social Workers,* Heinemann, London.

Doyle, D. (1980). Home care for the dying. *Geriatric Medicine,* **10** (7), 4-5.

Jones, B. (1967). *Design for Death,* André Deutsch, London, p. 25.

Kamisar, Y. (1978). *Ethical Issues in Death and Dying,* Prentice Hall, Englewood Cliffs, N.J.

Mann, T. (1924). *The Glass Mountain,* quoted in *Bartlett's Familiar Quotations,* Macmillan Press, London.

Martin, A. (1980). The law and the nurse. 'A right worth dying for'. *Journal of Community Nursing,* **4** (6), 25-26.

Morrice, J. K. W. (1976). *Crisis Intervention,* Pergamon Press, Oxford.

Saunders, C. (1965). Telling patients. *District Nursing,* **8**, 149.

Pine, V. (1975). *Caretakers of the Dead,* Irvington, New York, and John Wiley, New York.

Suicide Act 1961, HMSO, London.

Trowell, H. (1973). *The Unfinished Debate on Euthanasia,* SCM Press, London.

Whitehead, T. (1974). *Psychiatric Disorders in Old Age,* Harvey, Miller and Medcalf, London.

9 Into the Future

We should all be concerned about the future because we are all
going to have to spend the rest of our lives there

C. F. Kettering (see *Bartlett's Quotations*)

Introduction

What has the future to offer the retired and the about to be
retired? Modern gerontology tells us that there will be more
of us, as a percentage of the population, entering that stage
of life up to the end of the century than the country has
ever had to cope with before. This chapter looks forward to
the changes which we might achieve in the future. We will be
better educated and more vocal than our predecessors. We
will be slightly better off financially — adding to our political
strength. There will be more flexibility about retirement
age, and less discrimination. Medical and technological
advances will mean that the quality as well as the quantity
of life will improve. The notion of the retired as un-people —
unable, unemployable, uninteresting and unadaptable —
should change as the retired themselves organise and demand
their rightful place in society.

Those who view retirement with dread and apprehension,
thinking that the good days are over, should take a leaf out
of Harry's book:

Driving past a pub one day at chucking out time, I saw
Harry and his disreputable old dog stagger out. Harry was
well over 80 and the dog was equally elderly in canine
terms. They were both not quite drunk, but definitely
merry. It was a good mile and a half to their home and as
I was going that way I gave them a lift. The smell of beer
from Harry and of halitosis and beer from the dog made
me wish I had minded my own business.

'Why do you drink so far from home, Harry?' I asked.

'Because the beer's good there. Best beer I've ever tasted,' he belched all over me.

'I thought you told me you could never find a beer as good as in the old days,' I reminded him.

'If I did, me darling, I lied. I'll tell you about the good old days. The only good thing about the good old days was that nobody interfered. My father could kick the hell out of my mother and us kids every week when he got drunk and nobody interfered. My poor old mother died from undernourishment and overwork when she was 49 and nobody interfered. When she was lying dead in the bed my drunken old sot of a father came home drunk and climbed into the bed beside her and went to sleep and none of us had the courage to interfere. There was only three of us left at home by then. I was the youngest, 14 I was. We thought, there's nothing we can do for our poor old mother, so we all left home that night and hoped that when he woke up the next morning he'd get the shock of his life.'

'And did he?' I asked.

'Don't know, we never went back. Never saw the old b. . . . . . . again. An aunt of mine got me a job in a printing works and they let me sleep in an empty attic room. I worked from eight in the morning to eight at night. That's what the good old days were all about, me darling.' Harry was waxing to his theme and my head was getting quite light with the second-hand fumes of alcohol and halitosis.

'Why do you give the dog so much beer, Harry? I'm sure it's not good for him.'

'Because he likes it, me darling, and it's his tricks that gets us the free beer, so it's only fair that he should have his share.' Harry laughed deafeningly at the contemplation of his own joke, 'Being a good manager, I take 90 per cent and he gets 10 per cent.'

I suddenly had a fellow feeling with the dog. This was obviously the reason they moved around the pubs, fresh audiences and more beer. We had arrived outside their home.

'You're home, Harry. Get out and take that revolting old drunk with you.' He was laughing so much I had to help him and the scruffy old mongrel out of the car.

'Today is the good day, me darling. Today and tomorrow and all the tomorrows after that. The past is dead, but we're

not. Thanks for the lift, me darling.'
They both staggered up the path and into the house.

So much for the 'good old days'. Like Harry, I don't believe in them. The past is gone. Nothing can change our old mistakes, blunders, indiscretions or transgressions. Not even God can alter the past, only the historians can do that. The future — now that's something else again; the future is ours, no matter what age we are. The future can be moulded. The only good we get from the past is knowledge — not to make the same mistakes again.

Health in the Future

> If I'd known I was going to live so long, I'd have taken better care of myself
>
> Leon Eldred (see Peter, 1977)

Modern geriatric medicine is increasingly energetic, alive and effective. It aims at mobility with stability. The emphasis is on rehabilitation and returning home. It does not, however, remove from the individual the responsibility of caring for his or her own health. Ultimately we are all responsible for our own lives. What good geriatric care does is to offer the facilities for preventative health education, easy referral, accurate diagnosis and early treatment. We must get away from the assumption that all aches and pains in the elderly are due to 'old age'.

'I can't walk to the shops any longer, it's the pain in my feet.'

'What sort of pain?'

'Just old age, I suppose,' this old friend of mine said, producing two grossly swollen and odematous legs.

The old adage that 'What can't be cured must be endured' may have its point, but at least let's try to find the cure first. Gross under-reporting of ill health in the elderly is a well established fact, so what we should be looking for is early referral and early treatment.

Preventative geriatric medicine should have as its prime objective the mental, physical and social well-being of the retired population. Good health does not mean just an absence of disease. It is a more positive concept than that and it is interrelated with and depends on good housing, good finances, good social conditions and a good and satisfying environment.

HEALTH EDUCATION

Health education seeks to alter attitudes, but before we can alter other people's attitudes we must do a bit of altering ourselves. Use and abuse of tobacco, alcohol and drugs are not unknown in the medical, nursing and paramedical professions! There is nothing quite as ludicrous as a ponderous and over-weight doctor or nurse telling a patient they must loose weight. We happily go on accepting sponsorships from tobacco companies for sporting and other events, knowing that the advertising involved may well start other people on the road to lung cancer.

The future will undoubtedly bring more emphasis to education and prevention. Hypothermia, obesity, heart disease, accidents and drug abuse are already receiving fairly wide notice. Immunisation against influenza, screening clinics, and the use of age/sex registers in GP teams are all helping to keep the elderly healthy, but there is still much to do. More elderly people are disabled by the lack of suitable spectacles and wellfitting dentures than by crippling diseases. Many more are immobilised by the lack of a chiropody service than by other locomotive disorders.

THE NEED FOR RESEARCH

There will be more basic research into the biology of ageing. Butler (1979) talks of the research needed into Alzheimer's disease, into immunology and why the body loses its natural resistance with old age, and into endocrinology and hormonal change and their effects on osteoporosis and fractured hips.

Every day we see new advances in drug therapy. Drugs such as L-DOPA, oral diuretics, steroids, beta-blockers, tranquillisers, and antidepressants are all fairly recent advances which have helped change many lives, and no doubt the drug companies will continue to produce new drugs to improve the quality of life for us all. Dr Gerard Vaughan, speaking at the opening of the British Pharmaceutical Conference in September 1981, said that the future would see more people treated at home rather than in hospital: 'The new drugs of the 1980s will almost certainly consist of the products of advanced biotechnology by genetic engineering rather than today's production by synthetic chemistry.'

Research in the future can be expected to give us more knowledge on the rate of absorption and toxicity of drugs in older people. There could well be an extension of the use of paediatric/geriatric (PG) dosage. Illness in old age is different to that in the young. Older people have many more of the 'fits, faints and funny turns' types of illness. The inaccurate use of drugs could well account for some of them.

PRACTICAL HELP IN ILL-HEALTH

There are many good schemes and ideas in the embryo stage and the future will undoubtedly see them come to fruition. Perhaps one of the best is the suggestion that the DHSS should run its own nursing homes. There are many people now in hospital as long stay patients, blocking much needed and highly expensive hospital beds, which they neither want nor need. It would be much better for both the patient and the economy if they could be transferred to small friendly nursing homes run by the DHSS. Family, relatives and friends could help with their general care in these small units if they wished to. It is easier to take a relative out of a small unit of this type for the day than it is from a hospital ward. There is no reason why the family should not tuck the patient into bed when they do bring him or her back in the evening, and no reason why they should not take him or her out in a wheelchair to the hairdresser or to the park for an hour or so.

Most elderly patients do not need high technology care, they need loving, sympathetic and listening care. This could be better provided in small homely units, as long as they are properly organised and supervised.

The second use for this type of accommodation is that of half-way house. Many elderly people who live alone are discharged from hospital to empty homes. One day they are receiving full time care and the next they are on their own in an empty house. A DHSS nursing home would act as a half-way environment, to give them a chance to organise themselves while still having some supervision and minimal care. It would be particularly useful for the many elderly people who are taken to the accident and emergency departments of hospitals after falls in the street. Unless they have broken a leg it is unlikely that they will be admitted. However, it is not unusual for community staff to find very elderly people, perhaps several days later, in shock, pain and distress, their one good arm in plaster, and not able to wash, dress or cook.')

Another scheme being tried in some areas is a home aides scheme. Elderly people, on discharge from hospital, are given free use of an aide who will give short term intensive support. This support is usually given for a week or two until the elderly person has got the confidence and ability to cope on their own with normal cover from the home help service.

In some districts the incontinence laundry service has been extended to include a sheet exchange scheme worked in conjunction with the hospital laundry. Soiled and wet sheets are put into plastic sacks and are collected twice a week in exchange for an agreed number of clean sheets.

Night sitting services are supplied by some authorities and may well be extended. Families could cope better with terminally ill members if they had an occasional night of uninterrupted sleep. It not only gives them a rest, but the support of knowing that society realises the strain and stress of the situation.

Retirement in the Future

> Work is something you do so that sometime you won't have to do it any more
>
> Alfred Polgar (see Peter, 1977)

Much of the literature on gerontology takes a very dismal and apprehensive view of retirement. It points to the loss of role and status, to the reduced finances, to the loss of dignity and the feeling of being needed. It talks of people being discriminated against because of age, and retirement is seen as compulsory unemployment or as death to personality. Personally I can no more subscribe to these fears than I can to the illusion of 'the good old days'. Nobody is going to cast a blight over my retirement. I've earned it, I'm looking forward to it and by golly, I'm going to enjoy it.

One of the great things about retirement is that you have finished striving for position. You no longer have to be very careful of what you say in case the boss, manager or shop steward is listening. You can say what you like, do what you like, take more chances, be more adventurous. You can give people the benefit of your opinion whether they want it or not. Yes, we will get more wrinkles, more arthritis, gradually slow down, but the brain, which is the most important organ in the body, does not get wrinkles or arthritis. As long as we do not become afflicted with the dreaded dementia and we can keep our mental faculties, that is all that matters. I see retirement not as the end, but as the beginning of a new life.

TRAINING FOR RETIREMENT

In the future training for retirement will become more necessary as the number of people reaching the age of retirement increases and their life expectancy lengthens. 'At present, only about six per cent of people approaching retirement receive any formal preparation' (HMSO, 1981). We all need to come to terms with major changes in our lives. With retirement we may have to face social, psychological and financial changes. Those who have been through a learning process to prepare them for this adjustment have had what the psychologists call 'anticipatory guidance', and they will react and come to terms better with their new life-style.

The belief that employers have a duty and a responsibility beyond retirement is gaining ground. Many large firms have clubs, newsletters and personnel staff to keep people in touch with each other and with the firm. However, many more firms and certainly all government departments should show a lead and extend the number of retirement courses they offer to their staff.

A retirement course should not only tell people what their pension is going to be and how to invest their money — if they have any — but how to maintain optimum health, vigour and interest. It should point out what further education is available in the way of adult educational courses, Open University courses and training courses for those caring for elderly relatives. Education in retirement should never be seen as a time-filling endeavour, but as a stimulating, enjoyable seeking of knowledge.

A good course should include discussion on possible future work, be it part time, casual or voluntary. Housing, leisure and budgeting should also be discussed. Above all it should make people think seriously, perhaps for the first time, about the changes they will have to make and how they and their family are going to adjust to them.

WORK IN RETIREMENT

At present many people do a little work in retirement. Some do part time or sessional work at their own jobs, others do a little gardening, domestic or casual work. It is not unusual to find people unaware of the 'earnings rule'. This applies to anyone in receipt of a retirement pension who earns money by employment which is above a set figure (in 1981 this was £52 per week). If they earn more than the set figure their pension is reduced on a sliding scale. This applies to men up to 70 and women up to 65 years. It not only discourages some people from working, but makes others dishonest by not declaring their earnings, and these undesirable aspects of the law really should be removed.

The idea of a flexible retirement age, both up and down the scale, is also gaining ground. Part time work for a few years before full retirement is reached is already in evidence in some European countries. Sweden now runs a Partial Pension Scheme which allows people to retire gradually. Swedish people are entitled to their state retirement pension at age 65. The Partial Pension Plan starts at 60 years of age and operates until recipients are 70, allowing the individual to work part time and draw a partial pension. The future should see more experimentation in this field.

VOLUNTARY/COMMUNITY WORK

Voluntary work should not be a one-way process. In the future we should not just think only of what society can do for the retired and the elderly, but what the retired and elderly can do for society. Already we have numerous young and not so young retired people working in the voluntary field, bringing to this work skills, expertise and a life-time of experience. People who give their time in the service of others gain a lot of satisfaction and they become a life-line to those they serve. Examples abound:

'To know that twice a week I can go out for two whole hours without worrying if John is setting fire to himself or the house is luxury.'

'The street Warden saw my card in the window and he came in and got the doctor and I was sent to hospital, otherwise I think I would have died.'

'The boys from the local school did my garden.'

'Since my eyesight has got so bad, Joan reads my letters and sees to my pension and all that. I don't know what I'd do without her.'

'I read about this scheme in America where they had Foster Grans for handicapped children and children in hospital, and one day my Stephen, who is 6, asked where his granny was and I had to tell him he didn't have one because my mother is dead and so is Tom's. So on the spur of the moment I advertised in the local paper for a foster granny and I got eight answers. Now Stephen has two Grans, Granny Morris and Granny Evans. They have become good friends to us and to each other. Stephen is delighted. Tom says I'm mad, but he thinks it's a hoot. He calls one his foster mother and the other his foster mother-in-law.'

What could be nicer for some children who have not got a grandmother than to have a Foster Gran, because according to some 6 year olds I asked, Grannys are: 'ever so nice'; 'fat but lovely'; have blue hair and teeth that come out'; 'always have chocolate biscuits'; 'knit jumpers that are too big'; 'let you drive the cows on the farm'; 'are almost as old as me'; like the children's programme on the telly'; 'can't hear you because their ears go to sleep'.

The Good Neighbour Campaign in which the street warden or link person displays an emblem in their window to indicate their willingness to help, and makes personal contact with every person in the street, can be a great assistance to the elderly, disabled and isolated. They can rally support in times of crisis, distribute health education literature, and be a point of contact for all the statutory services. The scheme could well be extended with training for the link person and perhaps payment of an honorarium to offset their out of pocket expenses.

There are literally thousands of voluntary jobs available to those who have a little time to offer. Most hospitals, social services departments and charity groups are crying out for voluntary workers. Volunteer bureaux can now be found in most towns and cities and enquiries are always welcome. The future will see a great extension of voluntary work as the needs of the elderly increase faster than the country's financial ability to meet the needs.

Housing in Retirement: Future Requirements

The majority of retired people stay in their own homes, but there is always a proportion who move. The move may not be of their own making, but forced upon them because they are in 'tied housing'. The accommodation goes with the job and when the job finishes so does the accommodation. Farm workers, school caretakers and people who have 'living-in' jobs like hotel workers and nurses in hospital accommodation, even ministers of religion have these problems. For them retirement can be very traumatic because they have the added difficulty of finding a new home.

For the others who move, it may be that they wish to move nearer their family or to join the exodus to the south coast. They would do well to stop and consider the difficulties they may face in losing the familiar patterns of life for what is only a *supposedly* better pattern. The south coast towns may be warmer, but they have their dreary winters just like every other place. Younger families may themselves move, leaving the older generation behind in a strange town. The financial cost of moving is now quite considerable and new places usually require such expenses as new carpets and curtains, adding to the financial strain. Moves should never be the result of quick decisions, they need thought, agreement by all the parties concerned and a great deal of preparation.

It is to be hoped that the future will see a lot more building by the housing associations, charities and local authorities of warden-controlled flats and flatlets for the elderly. There is great scope for the extension of the concept of residential clubs, rather than old folks' homes. There is a possibility of foster homes for the elderly on the same principle as foster homes for children. It could be particularly important for ethnic groups and long stay patients in mental hospitals who are capable of being rehabilitated back into the community.

There is a great need to educate the public into accepting more half-way homes for the mentally ill and handicapped in residential areas. We need more local authority grants for improving and adapting homes. The idea of the granny flat is gaining ground, but it is still very much a middle-class ethic, probably because it requires a fair amount of money to build on to the family home, but it is something that the housing associations could well consider for the future.

Poverty and Finance

The greatest of evils and the worst of crimes is poverty
George Bernard Shaw (see Peter, 1977)

There are some very basic facts to accept when we retire. One is that nobody is as well off financially in retirement as they were when in full time employment, but sorting out the budget helps. The second point to remember is that nobody gets an Old Age Pension, we get a State Retirement Pension and we get it because we have paid insurance contributions all our working lives. Elder (1977), speaking of the label says, 'It has a wholly working-class connotation, with over-tones suggesting that OAPs are the recipients of philanthropy — the Welfare State grandiosely distributing alms to the maimed and the old.' The third point to remember is that there are millions of pounds worth of unclaimed benefits, particularly supplementary pensions, so that always when dealing with the elderly we should ask about their finances; always press them to apply to the DHSS and give a life-line so that they don't feel guilty about coming back if nothing happens; something like, 'If you don't hear anything in three weeks, come back and I will follow it up.'

Throughout the literature on ageing there is not only strong condemnation of the conditions which create poverty and need, but also an acknowledgement that poverty still exists in our affluent society. Only by improving pensions will we eliminate poverty in that most vulnerable group — the elderly. Dignity becomes easier with a full belly and paid-up bills.

Retirement and the Family

The family is the nucleus of civilisation

W. Durant (see Peter, 1977)

Few people retire alone. When the husband retires, the wife

also retires. She too must alter her way of life. After a few weeks, the initial holiday feeling will wear off and the thought that she must now have him under her feet for the rest of their lives will leave her with a lot of adjusting to do. Forward planning, talking about it, realigning household chores, changing the daily pattern a little here and there and retaining a sense of humour about it will help to make the transition a peaceful and enjoyable one.

As people become more aged and dependent, younger members of the family may be called upon to help. Research has shown that families do respond to requests for help with love and devotion within the limits of their ability. Even when the distance between the nuclear and extended family is great, there is frequent contact by letter and telephone. The support supplied will also depend on the type of relationship that exists between the older and younger generations. Not all parents have been good, caring people themselves — we tend to reap what we have sown. Stress factors also affect people differently. To those who only need a little sleep, broken nights caring for elderly relatives do not present great hardship. On the other hand, some people can be absolutely shattered after a couple of sleepless nights and be on the point of collapse. Proper financial and practical support to the family by the statutory agencies could well make all the difference between their ability to cope and the elderly person going 'into care'. Old people are seldom 'far better off in a home.'

Rights of the Individual

We all have certain inalienable rights: the right to free speech, the right to work, the right to practise our religious beliefs. We also have the right to think of our homes as sacred and beyond the interference of any outside agency. These rights do not cease to matter as we grow older; on the contrary, the right to remain in one's own home without unwarranted interference may become very important to an older person.

We have a right to dignity and to freedom from hunger. We have a right to our given name; depriving us of that deprives us of our dignity and self-esteem. We are not everybody's Gran.

The dying also have rights. They have the right to expect us to listen to them and allow them to talk and to answer their questions truthfully. It is, after all, a fairly big thing in our lives and it only happens once; we may all like to say a few words about it before we go. For years we thought that the dying did not know they were dying, but then again, for years we thought the world was flat.

Above all we have the right to be seen as an individual, whatever our age, sex, colour or creed. We are all people first, with an ordinary person's ability to live, love and pursue our own particular type of happiness. Some of the great 'individuals' of this century have left us gems of their very individual and unique contribution to to-day's society. As the quotations in Appendix 1 show, they had the ability to express what perhaps the majority of us feel.

Conclusions

We must all grow old, that is inevitable, but with his instinct for survival, man will forever seek to delay the process. He will go to great lengths on the trail of rejuvenation. There will always be followers of new fads — diets, elixirs, potions, meditation, exercises and so on, but so far nobody has stayed around long enough to prove that they work. Old age may have its regrets, as all ages have, but it need have no fear for us as long as we have made society aware that we refuse to be penalised just because we've grown old. To all those who are about to retire and to all those already retired, the message is 'look to your rights, be vocal, be heard, do not accept the second best'. The important thing is 'that you live all the days of your life'. During those days, make people aware of your individuality. Do not allow anyone to treat you as an ex-person. We all have a place in the scheme of things; we all deserve our place in the sun. Make sure that your place is of your own choosing and that everyone knows and respects your choice. Remember, retirement is a beginning — not an ending.

References

Bartlett's Quotations, Macmillan Press, London.

Butler, R. (1979). The graying of nations, *Age Concern Occasional Paper No. 6.*

HMSO (1981). *Growing Older*, HMSO. London.

Elder, G. (1977). *The Alienated*, Writers and Readers Publishing Co-operative, London, and Macdonald and Evans, London.

Peter, L. (1977). *Quotations for Our Time*, Methuen Paperbacks, London.

Suggested Reading

Comfort, A. (1976). *A Good Age*, Crown Publishing, New York.

DHSS (1977). *A Happier Old Age: A Discussion Document on Elderly People in our Society*, HMSO, London.

HMSO (1981). *Growing Older, HMSO*, London.

Puner, M. (1974). *To the Good Long Life*, Macmillan Press, London.

Riessman, F. (ed.) (1977). *Older Persons — Unused Resources for Unmet Needs*, SAGE Publications, New York.

Hobman, D. (ed.) (1978). *The Social Challenge of Ageing*, Croom Helm, London.

Appendix 1: Some Magnificent Examples of Old People

People who have grown old with wisdom, still working, producing, conducting, painting, splendid in their age, radiant, brilliant people — an example to us all:

Eleanor Roosevelt, 1884-1962
'No-one can make you feel inferior without your consent.'

Sophie Tucker, 1884-1966
'I have been poor and I have been rich. Rich is better.'

Charles Chaplin, 1889-1977, who married again at 54 years old and had eight children and at the age of 75 said,
'My life is more thrilling today than it ever was.'

Albert Schweitzer, 1875-1965
'The tragedy of life is what dies inside a man while he lives.'

Henry Ford, 1863-1947
'Anyone who stops learning is old, whether at twenty or eighty. Anyone who keeps learning stays young. The greatest thing in life is to keep your mind young.'

Mark Twain (Samuel Clemens), 1835-1910, who sent the following famous cable from London to Associated Press:
'The reports of my death are greatly exaggerated.'

Bob Hope, 1903-
'You know you're getting old when the candles cost more than the cake.'

Bertrand Russell, 1872-1970
'To fear love is to fear life, and those who fear life are already three parts dead.'

Margaret Kuhn, 1904-   leader of the Gray Panthers, named after its members' hair colour
'We are not mellowed, sweet old people. We're outraged, but we're doing something about it.'
'The trouble with America is the Detroit syndrome. We only want the latest models.'

Winston Churchill, 1874-1965
'When I look back on all those worries I remember the story of the old man who said on his deathbed that he had had a lot of trouble in his life, most of which had never happened.'

Pablo Picasso, 1881-1973
'I'd like to live like a poor man with lots of money.'

George Bernard Shaw, 1856-1950
'The worst sin towards our fellow creatures is not to hate them, but to be indifferent to them; that's the essence of inhumanity.'

Pope John XXIII, 1881-1963
'It often happens that I wake at night and begin to think about a serious problem and decide I must tell the Pope about it. Then I awake completely and remember that I am the Pope.'

Appendix 2: Useful Voluntary Agencies and Addresses

Abbeyfield Society, 35a High Street, Potters Bar, Hertfordshire EN6 5DL. Tel. Potters Bar (0707) 43371.
Housing units for fit and healthy elderly persons.

Age Concern (Headquarters), Bernard Sunley House, 60 Pitcairn Road, Mitcham, Surrey CR4 3LL. Tel. 01-640 5431.
Runs day centres, clubs, training courses. Over 100 branches throughout the country.

Alcoholics Anonymous, 11 Redcliffe Gardens, London SW10 9BG. Tel. 01-352 9779.

Al-Anon Family Groups, 61 Great Dover Street, London SE1 4YF.
Support groups for the friends and relatives of problem drinkers.

British Association for Retired Persons (BARB), 14 Frederick Street, Edinburgh.
Information on activities and ways retired people can help themselves.

British Diabetic Association, 10 Queen Anne Street, London W1M OBD.

British Red Cross Society, 9 Grosvenor Crescent, London SW1X 7EJ. Tel. 01-235 5454.
Provides aids and transport for sick persons. Also has an aftercare service.

British Rheumatism and Arthritis Association, 6 Grosvenor Crescent, London SW1X 7EH.
Welfare service, holiday home, information on aids.

The Church Army (Headquarters), Independents Road, Blackheath, London SE3 9LG. Tel. 01-318 1226.
Provides holiday homes for the aged.

Council of Social Services for Wales, Crescent Road, Caerphilly, Mid-Glamorgan. Tel. Caerphilly (0222) 86224/6

Counsel and Care for the Elderly (Elderly Invalids' Fund), 131 Middlesex Street, London E1 7JF. Tel. 01-621 1624.
Advice on anything concerning the elderly. Grants for needy chronic invalids.

Citizens Advice Bureau — see local telephone directory

Cruse (The Organisation for Widows and their Children) (Headquarters), 126 Sheen Road, Richmond, Surrey. Tel. 01-940 4818.

Distressed Gentlefolks' Aid Association, Vicarage Gate House, Vicarage Gate, London W8. Tel. 01-229 9341.
Pensions, financial help and clothing

Friends of the Elderly and Gentlefolks' Help, 42 Ebury Street, London. Tel. 01-730 8263.
Financial help to the elderly. Will sometimes help with nursing home fees.

Help the Aged, 32 Dover Street, London W1A 2AP. Tel. 01-499 0972.
Sheltered housing, day centres. Care for the aged throughout the world.

Incontinence Advisory Service, The Disabled Living Foundation, 346 Kensington High Street, London, W4. Tel. 01-602 2491.

Jewish Welfare Board, 315/317 Ballards Lane, London N12 8LP. Tel. 01-446 1499.

Methodist Homes for the Aged, 11 Tufton Street, London

SW1P 3QD. Tel. 01-222 0511.

National Benevolent Fund for the Aged, 12 Liverpool Street, London EC2. Tel. 01-283 3287.
Financial and holiday help.

The National Council on Alcoholism, 3 Grosvenor Crescent, London W1X 7EL. Tel. 01-235 4182.

National Council for the Single Woman and Her Dependents, 29 Chilworth Mews, London W2 3RG. Tel. 01-262 1451. Advice and support for those who care for an elderly relative at home.

National Council for Voluntary Organisations, 26 Bedford Square, London WC1. Tel. 01-636 4066.
Will supply addresses of volunteer bureaux and Councils for Voluntary Services nationwide.

National Federation of Old Age Pensions Associations, Melling House, 91 Preston New Road, Blackburn, Lancashire B2 6BD. Tel. Blackburn (0254) 52606.

Northern Ireland Council of Social Service, 2 Annadale Avenue, Belfast. Tel. Belfast (0232) 650011/2/3.

Pre-Retirement Association of Great Britain and Northern Ireland, 19 Undine Street, Tooting, London SW17 8PP. Tel. 01-767 3225.

Presbyterian Residential Trust, Church House, Fisherswick Place, Belfast BT1 6DW. Tel. Belfast (0232) 22284.

Professional Classes Aid Council, 10 St Christopher's Place, London. Tel. 01-935 0641.
General relief for professionals and their dependents in distress for whom statutory or other voluntary help is not available.

Retirement Association of Northern Ireland, 42 Botanic

Avenue, Belfast BT7 1JQ. Tel. Belfast (0232) 21324.

Royal British Legion, 49 Pall Mall, London, SW1W 5JY. Tel. 01-834 9353.
Help for ex-servicemen and women and their dependents.

Royal United Kingdom Beneficent Association, 6 Avonmore Road, London. Tel. 01-602 6247.
Help for professional people over 65, or disabled people over 40.

St John Ambulance Association and Brigade (Headquarters), 1 Grosvenor Crescent, London SW1X 7EF. Tel. 01-235 2531.
Day centres, clubs for the elderly, help with transport, visits to the aged and disabled at home.

Salvation Army (Headquarters), 101 Queen Victoria Street, London EC4 4EP. Tel. 01-236 7020.

The Scottish Council of Alcoholism, 47-49 York Place, Edinburgh EH1 3JD. Tel. 031-556 0459.

Scottish Council of Social Services, 18/19 Claremont Crescent, Edinburgh EH7 4D. Tel. 031-556 3882.

Shaftesbury Society, Shaftesbury House, 112 Regency Street, London SW1. Tel. 01-834 2656.
Holiday centres in Whitstable and Dover.

Society of St Vincent de Paul, 24 George Street, London W1 5RP. Tel. 01-935 7625.
Mainly Catholic. Helps all in need. Visits to poor and old in hospital and at home.

Samaritans (Headquarters), 17 Uxbridge Road, Slough, Berks. Tel: Slough (0753) 32713.
24 hour free confidential telephone counselling for the suicidal, distressed and despairing. Local branches in most areas.

Shelter, 157 Waterloo Road, London SE1. Tel. 01-633 9377.
Advice and information on housing matters.

Scottish Old Age Pensions Association, 12 Gordon Street, Lochgelly, Fife PY5 9PT.
Co-ordinates pensioners' organisations in Scotland.

Society for the Assistance of Ladies in Reduced Circumstances, Lancaster House, 25 Hornyold Road, Malvern, Worcestershire. Tel. Malvern (068 45) 4645.
Monthly grants according to age and circumstances.

Task Force, Clifford House, Edith Villas, London.
Organises voluntary help in 10 London boroughs. Practical help to lonely and housebound.

Women's Royal Voluntary Services, 17 Old Park Lane, London W1Y 4AJ. Tel. 01-499 6040.
Meals on wheels, clubs, clothing and some aftercare services following discharge from hospital.